CONTENTS

Gaura Purnima I 3

Gaura Purnima II 9

Gaura Purnima III 16

Holi I 22

Holi II 27

Holi III 33

Rama Navami I 38

Rama Navami II 44

Rama Navami III 52

Narasimha Chaturdashi I 57

Narasimha Chaturdashi II 64

Narasimha Chaturdashi III 71

Krishna Janmashtami I 76

Krishna Janmashtami II 83

Krishna Janmashtami III 88

Vyasa Puja I 92

Vyasa Puja II 98

Vyasa Puja III 104

Radhashtami I 109

Radhashtami II	117
Radhashtami III	124
Dussehra I	127
Dussehra II	133
Dussehra III	140
Diwali I	144
Diwali II	149
Diwali III	155
Govardhana Puja I	159
Govardhana Puja II	165
Govardhana Puja III	172

Vaishnava Holidays

Krishna's Mercy

Copyright © 2012 Krishna's Mercy

All rights reserved.

www.krishnasmercy.org

INTRODUCTION

In celebrating glories of the Lord never to go too far,
And so many occasions for such in calendar year there are.

Chanting the holy names is the best way,
To fill the gap, to occupy the time in each day.

Nevertheless, anniversaries of significance give us a chance,
To remember even if we forget, our fortunes to enhance.

What follows is discussion of occasions I most prefer,
So certainly a complete list here I do not offer.

Gauranga, Narasimha, Prahlada, Radha, Sita and Rama come to mind,
From Diwali, Govardhana Puja and the guru's day auspiciousness to find.

GAURA PURNIMA I

Gaura Purnima celebrates the appearance day anniversary of Lord Shri Krishna Chaitanya Mahaprabhu, the most recent incarnation of Lord Shri Krishna, the Supreme Personality of Godhead, to appear on earth. Lord Chaitanya's most lasting contribution to humanity was His distribution of Krishna-prema, or love for God, to everyone He encountered. He spread Krishna consciousness throughout India at a time when most transcendentalists were dedicated to the monist philosophy of Shankaracharya.

The Vedas tell us that God can be realized in three distinct features: Brahman, Paramatma and Bhagavan. God's original feature is that of Bhagavan, or the Supreme Personality of Godhead. God then takes various incarnations and expansions in order to perform various tasks. The avatara, or incarnation of God, is a concept that the people of India are very familiar with. In olden times India was known as Bharatavarsha since it was ruled by King Bharata. Bharatavarsha actually referred to the entire world, for everyone lived in India during the early stages of creation. For this reason God's past incarnations usually appeared in India. This isn't to say that God, or Krishna, is the exclusive property of Indians. In fact the Shrimad Bhagavatam tells us that God's incarnations are too many to count, therefore the Vedas give reference to only the primary avataras.

Since God has an unlimited number of incarnations, we have seen many people appear in India over the past five thousand years who claimed to be expansions of Vishnu or Krishna. If they personally didn't declare they were God, then their followers did. Not only were great personalities declared to be incarnations of God, but many were also taken to be incarnations of great personalities of the past. Whether these people were bona fide incarnations or not is up for debate, but one thing we do know is that most of them expounded a philosophy other than devotional service, or bhakti-yoga. All great historical personalities appear for a specific purpose based on time and circumstance. Shankaracharya, for example, appeared during a time when the atheist Buddhist philosophy was very popular in India. Shankaracharya preached an impersonalist philosophy, whereby man was taken to be part of Brahman, and therefore considered to be equal to God. Later on, Vaishnavas like Ramanujacharya and Madhvacharya appeared to reestablish the supremacy of Lord Vishnu and to teach mankind that there is a difference between man and God.

We certainly owe a debt of gratitude to these saints, for they helped to clear up misconceptions that existed at the time. Yet there was still something missing in all these philosophies. To finally add the missing piece to the puzzle, Lord Krishna Himself had to appear on earth. As Lord Chaitanya, God came to firmly establish the discipline of bhakti-yoga, or devotional service, as the most bona fide method for transcendental realization. The quintessential teaching of the Vedas is that we are not this body. Our identity comes from the soul inside of us, and our body is a sort of temporary residence for the soul. Similar to how we can change apartments or houses based on our desires, our souls also can transmigrate between different bodies that can span many lifetimes. Throughout these changes, our identities don't change, but our outward appearance and material qualities do.

The soul's natural home is in the spiritual world. Temporary bodies can only exist in the material world. For a soul to remain here, it must accept a material body composed of gross and subtle elements. In the spiritual world, every person has a spiritual body which is full of bliss and knowledge. This is because God Himself is completely pure. Since the spiritual world is His home, it inherits all of His pure qualities. In order for our soul to return to its natural home, we must change our desires. Currently most of us have material desires which manifest through hankering and lamenting. Our mind is always hankering after things it wants and lamenting over things it doesn't have. Material life means always accepting or rejecting things. "I like this. I'm happy doing that. I hate this. I never want to suffer through that again." If we analyze the conversations that we have with others, we'd see that our statements usually fall into one of these categories. Spiritual perfection can be achieved when we no longer hanker nor lament.

This elevated state of mind is referred to as brahma-bhutah. Brahma refers to Brahman, or the impersonal energy expansion of God. Everything, both matter and spirit, is Brahman. Brahma-bhutah is the stage where one realizes that everything is Brahman, meaning that we are all equal constitutionally. This is true because no matter the type of body we currently possess, we are all spirit souls at our core. Our souls are actually separated expansions of Krishna. Krishna is the great soul, or Paramatma, and we are minute souls, jivatma. There is no difference in quality or quantity between jivatmas, meaning that all living entities are equal on a spiritual level. People who reach the brahma-bhutah platform of knowledge understand this non-duality that exists between living entities.

So how do we reach this elevated level of thinking? The Vedas give us several different methods which are all classified as yoga. Achieving union of the soul with God is known as yoga. All the great personalities that appeared in India over the past five thousand years propounded some version of yoga. Some proposed that people should analytically study the difference between matter and spirit, and use that knowledge to reach the brahma-bhutah platform. Others recommended the mystic yoga process, where one practices various breathing exercises and sitting postures as a way of mitigating the effects of the senses.

Many of these processes certainly are bona fide forms of yoga, but they are still subordinate to the highest discipline which is bhakti-yoga, also known as bhagavata-dharma or devotional service. Bhagavata refers to Bhagavan, or God, and dharma means occupational duty. Bhagavata-dharma, though classified as a religious system, is actually the natural occupation of the soul. Since spirit souls are personal expansions of God, it would make sense that any discipline that seeks to reconnect with the origin of the soul would be superior to any other religious system. Believing in God and wanting to serve Him is the natural inclination of all living entities. The other yoga systems, such as impersonal mental speculation and mystic meditation, are actually unnatural, and thus it is so rare to see people achieve perfection with these methods.

It is the natural inclination of man to believe in God and to love Him. Even young children take to God very easily, for they know that there is a higher power who is much stronger than they are. Though mankind has a natural affinity for devotional service, we still see that most people don't take to it as a way of life. This is because we need leaders to guide us. Most of us aren't trailblazers, meaning we won't go against the flow of society. If every person is occupied in karmic activity, it will be hard for those who are religiously inclined to take to devotional service. A strong leader is required who can set a path that can be followed by everyone else. This is precisely what Lord Chaitanya did. In the Bhagavad-gita, Lord Krishna tells us that He appears on earth from time to time to reinstitute dharma, or the principles of religion. In His appearance as Lord Chaitanya, God firmly established the supremacy of bhakti-yoga, or devotional service to God. Appearing in Mayapur, Lord Chaitanya was a great scholar in His youth. His name was Nimai Pandita, and He was so smart that He regularly defeated the great scholars of His time. Later on in life, however, He gave up mundane scholarship and took to the chanting of the maha-mantra, "Hare Krishna Hare Krishna, Krishna Krishna, Hare Hare, Hare Rama Hare Rama, Rama Rama, Hare Hare".

It wasn't that Lord Chaitanya gave up critical thinking or analytical study, but rather, He preached that logic and argument have limits. In a conversation He had with Sarvabhauma

Bhattacharya, and then later on with Sanatana Goswami, Lord Chaitanya expounded sixty-one different meanings to the famous atmarama verse in the Shrimad Bhagavatam. Lord Chaitanya's point was that the material world is full of dualities and that everything can be argued in a multitude of ways. What one person considers good, another person may consider bad, and vice versa. Instead of arguing things on the material level, Lord Chaitanya would explain everything in terms of Krishna, or God. Since one of Krishna's names is Achyuta, meaning the infallible one, it makes sense that any argument formed on the basis of Krishna's supremacy and infinite glories would also inherit the quality of infallibility.

Devotees like to visit temples, chant God's names, and read books about Him. Yet most societal leaders tell us that happiness in life comes through other activities such as economic development, sense gratification, or even philanthropy. Some spiritual leaders tell us that real perfection only comes through impersonal mental speculation or the performance of mystic yoga. Lord Chaitanya told us that not only is it okay to engage in devotional service, but that it should be our primary activity. It's okay to think about God all the time and to want to talk about Him with others.

Lord Chaitanya made it cool to be a devotee. We see that famous celebrities and musicians of today get the "rock star" treatment when they are in public. This refers to the large and raucous crowds that follow these celebrities around in public. In this regard, Lord Chaitanya was one of the greatest rock stars of all-time. He took to the renounced order of life, sannyasa, at only twenty-four years of age. Sannyasa is the last of the four Vedic ashramas, so those in the order are typically older than fifty years of age. Lord Chaitanya was very young, and usually younger people have a harder time being taken seriously. This wasn't the case with the Lord. He had a huge following of devotees wherever He went. People would marvel at the spontaneous display of affection and love He showed for Krishna, His name, forms, pastimes, and songs.

India has so many great temples that have existed for thousands of years. The events of the Ramayana and Mahabharata are known to almost all the citizens, thus there is a strong religious tradition that exists in the country. Lord Chaitanya tapped into the immense love for Krishna that existed naturally within all the citizens. Wherever He went, He asked people to simply chant Krishna's names, and to induce other people to chant. This simple formula led to a movement that swept through the country. Lord Chaitanya passed down the imperishable science of devotional service to His closest disciples, including the famous brothers Rupa and Sanatana Goswami. They both excavated Krishna's holy land of Vrindavana and erected many temples there. The spiritual leaders descending from Lord Chaitanya have produced volumes upon volumes of literature praising Lord Krishna and teaching others how to become pure devotees. These teachings have benefitted millions of people throughout the world.

Devotees can worship Lord Chaitanya and very quickly achieve liberation through His mercy. He is the same Krishna who appeared in Mathura some five thousand years ago. Devotees of any form of Lord Vishnu can take shelter of Lord Chaitanya, for He is the foremost teacher of vishnu-bhakti. Anyone who has ever chanted Hare Krishna in a pure way certainly has received the mercy of Lord Chaitanya, for He specifically recommended the chanting of this mantra in this age. On the auspicious occasion of Gaura Purnima, we remember the Lord and thank Him for all that He has done for us.

GAURA PURNIMA II

The glories of Shri Krishna Chaitanya Mahaprabhu can never be fully enumerated, but occasions such as Gaura Purnima, the celebration of His divine appearance, bring an added emphasis on remembering His transcendental activities and, more than anything else, another opportunity to bask in the light emanating from the golden sun of spiritual potency, the only hope for those otherwise blinded by the darkness of the age of Kali. Lord Chaitanya is an ocean of mercy that is full of transcendental nectar capable of deluging the entire earth with spiritual bliss by crossing any and all boundaries erected through nationalism, dogmatic insistence, and traditions based on narrow-mindedness or flat out ignorance. Indeed, there is no other form of Godhead more merciful, and proof of His divine nature and undying compassion is seen in His instructions, His pastimes and the glorious dedication to transcendental service instilled in His followers, who to this day carry the holy name of Shri Hari across the world to those who are desperately searching for ananda, or real bliss.

It is the nature of the spirit soul to crave supreme satisfaction; otherwise there would be no purpose to any activity. Every action is undertaken with a specific purpose, and upon careful observation a commonality is seen in all desires: ananda. Even something as simple as the removal of distress is rooted in the quest for pure bliss. Say, for example, that we own a car that is giving us trouble. Every week there seems to be a new problem. First the tires go bad, the next week the oil needs to be changed, and the week after that the transmission starts acting up. For those who have established a fixed routine for their daily activities, just one small slip up can cause a tremendous amount of distress. Taking the car into the repair shop results in being late to work and falling behind on the rest of the day's responsibilities. Owning a car also involves constant worry, as the solutions to problems aren't always readily available. As such, even when the car gets fixed, there is no guarantee that the issues will cease there.

The frustrated owner longs for the day when the automobile is either removed from their life or when it starts functioning properly on a regular basis. Though the impetus for activity, when viewed on an abstract level, seeks a remedy to a problem, the real driving force is the cherished desire for a peaceful existence. A worry-free life is one where ananda remains at high levels for extended periods of time. If we take the example of the car and expand it out to all activities, we'll see that bliss is at the core of every action in every form of life, even outside of the human form. Knowing that bliss is the central point of interest, wouldn't it be wonderful if we could find that one engagement related to a singular entity who can provide us more bliss than we've ever felt? Not surprisingly, the Supreme Lord, the fountainhead of all religious practice and the ideal beneficiary of every dedicated action, is meant to serve that very purpose.

When seeking out pleasure, the first instinct is to take service from another entity or object. "I want to satisfy my taste buds, so I'll go to a restaurant where a nice meal will be served up. I want to listen to some music, so I'll fire up a CD or an mp3 player filled with songs capable of bringing me tremendous, though albeit temporary, pleasure." But the most ideal relationship of a loving connection with the Supreme Lord actually works in the reverse way. God, who is known as Krishna in His original form, is all-blissful. In the imperishable land situated in the transcendental sky the source of all incarnations and everything spiritual and material simply plays His flute all day and does whatever He wants. This isn't to say that the only form of Godhead is Krishna, but rather, the most complete in terms of features and abilities is indeed Shyamasundara, the beautiful Lord having a blackish complexion.

Shri Krishna is the ultimate reservoir of pleasure, so His ananda never runs out. The individual fragments emanating from the Lord, we living entities, can tap into that storehouse of spiritual energy by engaging in Krishna's service. It is not that we have to approach the Lord and simply ask Him to share some of His blissful feelings with us. Rather, the sentiments towards performing unmotivated and uninterrupted service are naturally aroused from within when we adopt divine love, which manifests through activities such as chanting, hearing, remembering and worshiping. More than any other engagement, constant recitation of the holy names of the Lord found in the maha-mantra, "Hare Krishna Hare Krishna, Krishna Krishna, Hare Hare, Hare Rama Hare Rama, Rama Rama, Hare Hare", brings the pleasure of Krishna's association in the quickest amount of time. The chanting of Krishna's names also has the strongest effect on the consciousness, which needs to be purified in order to feel happiness at all times. The key to success is to regularly keep the divine vision, along with His names, attributes and pastimes, within the mind. Just as Krishna is all-attractive and always playing His flute, He also takes part in divine sports. If we have a penchant for activity, why should this behavior be absent in the most wonderful person the world has ever known?

The living entity is eternally a servant of Krishna. As such, only through the transcendental loving attitude can the storehouse of ananda be tapped in to. Through any other mindset, the individual living being, remaining forgetful of Krishna and the glorious nature of service to Him, must produce its own form of bliss through service to itself, the surrounding nature, or other beings not equal to God. Since none of these entities is all-attractive, they cannot even come close to providing the same pleasure that Krishna can. Therefore, the formula for finding eternal peace and happiness is to simply engage in Shyamasundara's service, in a mood tailored to the individual, without cessation.

The trouble is that not only is knowledge of the true mission of life unknown to most, but the very idea of God having a form and being ever worthy of worship through a loving attitude is not considered at all. If anything, the Almighty is viewed as an authority figure meant to be worshiped by those looking to acquire material rewards. Indeed, under this model, since the Lord is deemed to be angry and vengeful, neglect of His powerful position will bring about the severest of punishments. What gets overlooked in this belief system is that the living entity is already suffering, starting from the very moment that he searched for ananda in a realm bereft of Krishna's personal presence. Whether the acknowledgement of God's existence or a pledge of allegiance to a particular spiritual figure is made or not, the misery will continue for as long as consciousness remains unchanged.

The Vedas, the ancient scriptures of India, provide much detailed information about the nature of the Supreme Lord, His various forms, His pastimes and the need for the living entity to take to religion as a way of life, with the aim of steadily altering consciousness throughout the process. The thoughts of the mind at the time of death determine the nature of the next body assumed by the soul. If we think of God while quitting the body, we will attain a spiritual form in the next life. Any other consciousness brings about a renewed search for ananda that is doomed to suffer the same fate as that from the life just completed. Therefore, not wanting to risk rebirth and the renewal of the education process, sincere followers of the Vedic tradition follow strict rules and regulations aimed at purifying the thoughts of the mind. Aside from the assertive process of chanting the Lord's names, there are restrictions on the most sinful activities such as meat eating, gambling, intoxication and illicit sex.

Yet giving up sinful behavior, engagements which maintain the thick cloud of ignorance around the consciousness, is not an easy thing at all, especially when a particular society may be wholly accustomed to unauthorized behavior that mimics the animal community. Therefore another regulation voluntarily enforced by the aspiring transcendentalist of the Vedic school relates to association. The devotees of Krishna try to remain in the company of other devotees, for that will bring about the quickest progress in terms of altering consciousness. This certainly isn't a foreign concept. Young students attend school together, athletes train in groups, and businessmen meet at conventions and other formal gatherings to discuss ideas and to network. Spiritual life is the most intense of disciplines, so if bad association is maintained, the likelihood of remaining on the conditioned path, one that leads to the continuation of reincarnation, will increase.

When the recommended rules, regulations, and prohibitions on association are combined, there appears to be a stalemate, a seemingly insurmountable stumbling block towards achieving purification throughout a large section of society. If devotees are to avoid the association of the sinful, how will those not born into the Vedic tradition ever achieve purification? Should the Krishna bhaktas simply sit back and hope that others somehow figure out the right path in life? Maybe others will make advancement in their next birth, so there is no need to worry? These very concerns led to the advent of the greatest preacher the world has ever seen, a man who also happened to be non-different from Krishna Himself. Lord Chaitanya first graced this world with His divine presence on the auspicious occasion of Purnima in the month of Phalguna around five hundred years ago in the holy city of Navadvipa. The pastimes He would subsequently enact and the tradition of preaching He would leave behind would firmly establish Him as the most merciful entity this world has ever seen.

Though Lord Chaitanya was born a brahmana, which is the highest order in the varnashrama-dharma system instituted by the Vedas, His purpose was to preach the gospel of bhakti to all members of society, irrespective of their family lineage. Though speaking about the eternal truths of spiritual life found in sacred texts like the Bhagavad-gita to non-devotees is prohibited, Lord Chaitanya would not deny the mercy of Krishna bhakti to anyone. Rather than openly take to preaching amongst learned intelligentsia who were only interested in the intricacies of Vedanta philosophy, Shri Gaurahari approached the masses by travelling from village to village loudly reciting the holy names of the Lord. Through this sublime method, known as sankirtana, the mercy of Krishna and the holy name quickly spread throughout India.

Since devotees typically avoid situations and areas where the sinful element has a strong influence, areas bearing the opposite properties thus become places of pilgrimage. The banks of the holy river Ganges, or Ganga Devi, are filled with saintly people who always discuss the glories and pastimes of Shri Krishna and His other forms like Lord Rama, Vishnu and Narasimhadeva. But through Lord Chaitanya's tireless efforts, new places of pilgrimage sprung up, some in areas which were previously considered contaminated, as many new devotees were made after being induced to chant the holy name.

Not only did Lord Chaitanya inspire others to chant, dance and sing the names of Krishna and Rama, but He singlehandedly instituted a tremendously potent tradition of preaching that continues to this very day. His dear associates like Nityananda Prabhu went all across India and literally begged people to simply recite Krishna's name. It is not surprising to see the lengths of desperation that salesman will go to in order to make a sale of a car or insurance policy, for the benefit to them is financially related. After all, the man selling cars makes his living off getting others to purchase his product. But Nityananda Prabhu didn't want any money, or even any followers. His tremendously persuasive sales pitch was aimed at liberating others from the clutches of maya, or illusion.

Lord Chaitanya is so kind that if He sees that someone is already inclined towards worshiping Rama, Vishnu, or some other non-different form of Godhead, He will give them the knowledge to further increase their love and attachment. Evidence of this mercy is seen in the behavior of His followers who originally come from religious backgrounds not rooted in Vedic traditions. It is seen that Christians who take to Krishna-bhakti subsequently have a deeper and more profound love and respect for Lord Jesus Christ. Lord Chaitanya was an expert scholar in His youth, but He understood the limits to logic and argument. Rather than focus on word jugglery and logical proofs, Lord Chaitanya explained everything in terms of its relation to Krishna. As such, it is not surprising to see those who take to bhakti gain a firm understanding of the purposes behind all religions and the traits they share in common.

Shri Gauranga creates shelter with His very activities and teachings. Offering instructions and repeating do's and don'ts are one thing, but actually going out and rescuing those who are unaware of the true bliss to be found in bhakti represents a completely different level of benevolence and universal brotherhood. Lord Chaitanya and His associates drag those who are stuck in the mire of material existence into the light of bhagavata-dharma, or devotional service. As payback for their kind efforts, all that Shachinandana and His associates ask is that we remain committed to the chanting process, to glorifying the Supreme Lord and the spiritual master, and to never forgetting Krishna for even a moment.

On the wonderful occasion of Gaura Purnima, we remember Lord Chaitanya, who is the most merciful of teachers, the leader of the bhakti movement and the constructor of the sturdiest and most welcoming shelter this world has ever seen. May we worship Him for the rest of this lifetime and many more. Shri Chaitanya Mahaprabhu is Krishna Himself, so whoever honors Him will soon taste the most blissful holy name, a delight to be savored every day. Though Lord Chaitanya humbly asked that we give all our attention in worship to Shri Shri Radha and Krishna, we will never neglect service to Him nor will we ever forget His kind mercy. He is the umbrella protecting us from the harmful influences of the present age, and His associates and those who follow in His disciplic succession help to maintain that protection for all of humanity.

GAURA PURNIMA III

Lord Chaitanya is the preacher incarnation of Godhead who first made His mark on this earth some five hundred years ago in India, and His influence continues to spread across the world today. As the kindest saint, He had love and compassion for all creatures of the earth, and He sacrificed everything to spread the gospel of love and devotion to God to everyone, regardless of whether they gave a kind reception in return or not. If I know what others really need, what will bring them true happiness, wouldn't it be selfish of me to keep that knowledge confidential? Even if others scoff at my suggestions and curse me for my openness in speaking, shouldn't the nature of that knowledge trump whatever reactions I personally receive? In this way Shri Gaurahari is known as the most munificent incarnation of the Lord, for He gave love of God freely to everyone; something never before done.

Shrila Rupa Gosvami, soon to become one of the most famous saints of the bhakti tradition, once offered a very nice prayer to Lord Chaitanya, which addressed the fact that the son of mother Shachi and Jagannatha Mishra freely distributed prema for Lord Krishna, making Him more magnanimous than any previous incarnation. There are many avataras of the Supreme Personality of Godhead listed in the Vedic texts, and there are many unauthorized pseudo incarnations claiming divinity as well. Lord Chaitanya's divine nature is hinted at in the Mahabharata and Shrimad Bhagavatam, but His mission had nothing to do with making followers recognize His supremacy.

In the Bhagavad-gita, the original form of Godhead, Lord Krishna, explains that whenever there is a widespread discrepancy in the practice of religion, or dharma, and the rise of irreligion, He personally descends to earth. In the past this has meant Krishna appearing in some sort of fighting role, where a strong personality is defeated by divine weapons. Hiranyaksha was defeated by Lord Varaha, Hiranyakashipu by Narasimhadeva, Ravana by Lord Rama, and Kamsa by Krishna Himself. These enemies were originally devotees in the spiritual sky, but due to the will of Providence and the uncontrollable hand of fate, they made transgressions that caused their descent to the material world.

Only in a land full of duality can a previously devoted soul take on the opposite role of miscreant. These villains played their parts perfectly, and they were so vile that they caused the saintly class to petition for Krishna's direct intervention. So many tasks are carried out through Bhagavan's personal presence. With His various avataras, Krishna showed His splendid beauty, His immense strength, and His dedication to protecting the innocent. Since the events relating to these avataras are documented in the Puranas, Mahabharata, Ramayana and several other sacred texts, they can still be enjoyed to this day by people looking for the same protection that those persecuted in the past by the worst miscreants desired.

As Shri Gaurahari, Krishna appeared as a combined incarnation; both He and His pleasure potency together. The result was the Supreme Lord and His number one devotee taking on different moods at different times. The enemy this time was the seed of impurity implanted by the time period: Kali Yuga. Instead of using His tusks, fists, arrows, or nails, as Lord Chaitanya Krishna used the power of the holy name and its ability to melt the hardest hearts to defeat the enemy of impiety.

During Lord Chaitanya's time, medieval India, the mediums for mass distribution of information were not available. He could not broadcast the holy names in the maha-mantra, "Hare Krishna Hare Krishna, Krishna Krishna, Hare Hare, Hare Rama Hare Rama, Rama Rama, Hare Hare", through a radio signal. He could not record this sacred mantra, the greatest weapon against ignorance and deceit, onto a CD and then sell it through stores throughout the world. There was no internet and no television. With these conditions, obviously one would think the task of bringing large numbers of people to the cult of devotional service, the eternal and constitutional engagement of the spirit soul, would be impossible.

Yet just as the formidable Hiranyaksha was defeated by the strange form of a large boar, the veil of ignorance created by Kali

Yuga was no match for Shri Gaurahari, a mendicant without any material wealth. Hiranyakashipu tried to safeguard his life by receiving so many boons from Lord Brahma. He was not allowed to be killed in so many ways, but Krishna as Narasimhadeva foiled the demon's plans by killing him in just the perfect method. Ravana was similarly immune from all kinds of attack, so Bhagavan took the form of a human being to do away with him. Kamsa thought he was safe after killing so many innocent children of his sister Devaki, but Krishna can never be killed, and when He decides that someone else's time is up, nothing can be done to save them.

In the same way, the impediments of the time period were no match for Shri Gaurahari, who as a renounced mendicant went across India and infused the spirit of devotion into so many people. He did not go around the country giving people material gifts. He was not interested in distributing temporary wealth, though as the Supreme Lord He was capable of granting any benediction. He distributed something much more valuable: the holy name.

Why is this more valuable than tangible wealth? The holy name doesn't put food on the table. It doesn't pay the bills every month. It doesn't even give me any knowledge on how to earn a living. Ah, but these aspects of life essentially take care of themselves. If you had to, you could eat the fruits that fall off the trees. You could use simple rags for clothes and live in isolated caves. The animals can find the necessities of life without any problem, without any outside intervention. There are no welfare programs for the animals and no redistribution of wealth schemes to look after their welfare.

Krishna, through His impersonal energy of material nature, takes care of the needs of every living entity. Thus the real wealth one can find has nothing to do with matter. The holy name is the direct incarnation of Bhagavan, who is every single person's best friend. The ability to recite this name, to hold on to it for dear life, to take comfort in it, and to happily repeat it over and over again, is the real boon of the human form of life. Well aware of this, Lord Chaitanya tried to distribute that holy name to as many people as possible.

What would happen after someone met Lord Chaitanya? The devotional spirit would take over that kind-hearted soul. That spirit would then guide the rest of their activities. If I have a powerful torchlight, no matter how dark the environment may be, I can bring that light with me wherever I go and thus see whatever I need to see. With one light I can do so many other things. In a similar manner, with just one mantra, which contains the most potent names of Krishna and Rama, one can find a peaceful, enlivening, and enlightening activity under any circumstance.

Ideally, we would seek out a spiritual master, or guru, to get the confidential information of the Vedas. That knowledge is valuable because of its ability to positively effect change. At the same time, the guru doesn't want to openly distribute it to others, because not everyone will understand the information properly. Take one or two shlokas out of context and suddenly you have a worldwide movement trying to ban your system of religion. The mood of the worshiper must be proper; they must be humble and submissive in their learning. Only then will the power of the devotional path be revealed to them.

Lord Chaitanya was so merciful that He did not wait for others to approach Him. Through basic singing and dancing, the congregational style of chanting known as sankirtana, He brought the ancient art of divine love to anyone who was within audible range. He had a wife and family at home too, but for the good of humanity, He sacrificed personal pleasure. In favor of delivering the fallen souls looking for a real and legitimate religion to follow, Lord Chaitanya took sannyasa at a very young age and thus blazed the trail for future generations of preachers to follow.

Gaura Purnima celebrates Lord Chaitanya and His sublime mission. He was not on this earth for very long, but His influence is still felt to this day because of the sincere followers He inspired. His line of disciplic succession boasts some of the most intelligent, kind, and dedicated saints in history. Lord Chaitanya was not a sentimentalist. Though He preached primarily through chanting and dancing, that was just the best way to reawaken the devotional attitude in others. The foundation of that dedication in preaching was a keen understanding of Vedanta, the difference between matter and spirit, and the real meaning to religion.

With all that Lord Chaitanya sacrificed, what actually pleases Him? Aside from seeing others chant the names of Krishna and Rama in divine ecstasy, Lord Chaitanya's primary source of pleasure was hearing about Krishna. When He was in the bhava of Shrimati Radharani, Krishna's eternal consort, Shri Gaurahari felt the pains of separation from the darling of Vrajabhumi. Only when His closest associates would read poems from the likes of Jayadeva and Vidyapati would Lord Chaitanya feel some relief. His favorite Vedic text was the Shrimad Bhagavatam, for its sacred tenth canto has wonderful descriptions of Krishna's pastimes along with the prayers and heartwarming thoughts of the gopis of Vrindavana. Lord Chaitanya also preferred the Brahma-samhita and Krishna Karnamrita, two other works glorifying Krishna and devotion to Him.

Just as Gaurahari derived pleasure from hearing Krishna praised, so the sincere souls affected by Lord Chaitanya's preaching efforts take tremendous delight in hearing about His hearing about Krishna. Anyone who has ever chanted "Hare Krishna" or "Hare Rama" has enjoyed the mercy of Lord Chaitanya, who proclaimed those phrases to be the most powerful weapons against illusion in the Kali Yuga. His influence continues to this day through the hard work of His dedicated followers, those who appear in the line of disciplic succession that He made prominent. On Gaura Purnima, we remember that most merciful incarnation of Godhead and hope to always put a smile on His face with our chanting.

In Closing:

Chaitanya Mahaprabhu, of mother Shachi's delight,
Appeared on earth on day of full moon bright.

Would spread to the world wisdom's light,
At a time when irreligion at its height.

Message of divine love through sound was spread,

No difficult methods, chant holy names instead.

So many were pleased upon seeing Mahaprabhu,
His pleasure came from hearing about Krishna and gopis too.

For His honor names of Krishna and Rama we say,
Follow His path of bhakti day after day.

HOLI I

"Daityas, as truly as Vishnu is present in your weapons and in my body, so truly shall those weapons fail to harm me." (Prahlada Maharaja speaking to Hiranyakashipu's attendants, Vishnu Purana)

Holi is one of the most famous Hindu festivals celebrated each year. Known for its festive atmosphere, the playful throwing of colors on friends and family members, and singing and dancing, the holiday has its origin in religion and faith in God. Holi is named after the demon and sister of Hiranyakashipu, Holika. The annual occasion of Holi celebrates the thwarting of Holika's attempt at killing Hiranyakashipu's son, Prahlada.

Hiranyakashipu was a Daitya, or demon or asura, who ruled the earth millions of years ago. The Vedas provide a detailed lineage of man starting from the beginning of creation. There were two famous sisters, Diti and Aditi. The sons of Aditi became known as the Adityas, and they were all pious and devoted souls. The sons of Diti became known as the Daityas, and they were all demons by nature. Hiranyakashipu was a Daitya and a committed atheist. Similar to the Rakshasa demon Ravana, Hiranyakashipu performed great austerities for pleasing the demigods. They granted him several power augmenting boons and immunity from all sorts of enemies. Hiranyakashipu used these boons to terrorize the innocent, including the demigods. The demigods were so afraid of him that they would assume the guise of human beings and other species and then roam the earth incognito in hopes of avoiding Hiranyakashipu's wrath.

The Vedas tell us that there is only one God, Lord Krishna, ishvara parama krishna. The demigods, or devatas, are highly elevated living entities who manage various departments of the material creation. Essentially, the demigods are very powerful and one is advised to approach them if they are in need of any material benediction. Just seeing that the demigods were running around in fear is indication enough of how powerful Hiranyakashipu was. The demon was ruling over his kingdom when he had a son, whom he named Prahlada. The boy was the son of a Daitya, so Hiranyakashipu assumed that the child would worship him as his foremost deity. The Vedas tell us that the parents are the initial objects of worship for human beings, for the parents provide support and guidance during the early years of our life. Prahlada was certainly devoted to his father, but more so towards Lord Vishnu. Lord Krishna is the Supreme Personality of Godhead, and His primary expansion is Lord Vishnu. Krishna has two hands and Vishnu has four hands, but other than that, there aren't really any differences between the two forms. When discussing matters of devotion to God and the origin of man, the names of Krishna and Vishnu are interchangeable.

Prahlada was born a devotee due to the grace of Narada Muni. When Hiranyakashipu's wife was pregnant, Narada came and taught her about devotion to Krishna. The child in the womb, Prahlada, heard all this information and remembered it upon taking birth. This one fact alone teaches us so much. For expecting mothers, the best way to take care of the child in the womb is to listen to Krishna-katha, or talks or discourses about God. This will ensure that the child will grow up to be a devotee. If one is completely devoted to Krishna in this life, they will never have to suffer through birth and death again. In this way the mother can be an instrument for liberation. One of Lord Krishna's names is Mukunda, meaning one who grants mukti, or liberation. The Vedas tell us that the soul is eternal, but that the body is not. Once the soul departs from the body, it must continue to take repeated births for as long as it has material desires. Lord Krishna is the giver of mukti because only by thinking of Him at the time of death can we free ourselves from having to take birth again. By imbibing Krishna consciousness in the child while in the womb, the mother can jumpstart this liberation process.

As a child of only five years of age, Prahlada attended the gurukula, or school run by the spiritual master. When Prahlada would come home after school, Hiranyakashipu would ask his son what he learned. "Oh father, I learned that the supreme controller of all is Lord Vishnu. He is the greatest person of all, for everything in this world, both matter and spirit, emanate from him."

Hiranyakashipu became outraged after hearing this. He was a demon after all, so he didn't believe in a God. He thought that through fruitive activity and the performance of austerities that he himself had become the most powerful person in the world. He demanded that his son worship him instead of this Vishnu person. Prahlada kindly replied, "Oh father, there is no need to be angry. Lord Vishnu is inside of everyone, meaning He is inside of you as well. He is the benefactor of all creatures, so there is no reason to hold a grudge against Him."

Hiranyakashipu couldn't stand to hear this so he chewed out Prahlada's guru. The guru answered, "Oh demon, this boy hasn't learned these things from me. I haven't taught him anything relating to Vishnu, just those things necessary for running a kingdom." Prahlada went back to school but refused to change his ways. During recess, he lectured his classmates on the fleeting nature of material happiness, and how one can find true eternal bliss. "Lord Vishnu is the creator. Pleasing the senses only serves as temporary happiness, thus it is essentially useless. If we please the cause of all causes, we can gain liberation, meaning we will never have to suffer through this miserable existence in the material world." Again Hiranyakashipu questioned Prahlada as to what he had learned and again the boy replied, "Oh best of the asuras, know that Lord Vishnu is the greatest and that we should all be devoted to Him if we want to make our lives perfect." Prahlada was very keen, for he underhandedly insulted his father by calling him the best of the asuras. Demons loved to be praised, so Hiranyakashipu didn't understand that Prahlada was insulting him by calling him an asura, which is a demon or non-devotee. Not only that, but Prahlada referred to him as the greatest demon.

Hiranyakashipu decided to kill his son instead of hearing him praise Lord Vishnu. The best of the asuras was also worried that Prahlada would soon convince others to take up devotional service. This is the real reason the demons take to harassing the devotees. They simply don't like the fact that people worship God instead of them. All the oppressive governments of the world, past and present, operated on this principle. Hiranyakashipu tried every which way to kill his son, but none of them worked. He instructed his agents to attack his son with weapons, but as Prahlada mentions in the above referenced quote, none of those weapons could hurt him. Hiranyakashipu didn't give up, however. Prahlada was thrown off the cliff of a mountain, bitten by serpents, and thrown to the bottom of the river. Yet the boy survived all these attempts simply by focusing his mind on Lord Vishnu. While lying on the floor of the ocean, Prahlada was bound up and covered by rocks, yet simply by thinking of Lord Vishnu residing within the heart, Prahlada became one with God, in a sense. This is the power of devotion. Devotees understand that God is both one with and separate from the living entity. God is one with all of us in that He resides within our heart, right next to our soul. Perfection in life can be achieved by connecting with this feature of God, known as the Paramatma, or Supersoul. At the same time, Bhagavan is the source of the Supersoul, thus the living entities always remain subordinate. After connecting with the Supersoul, Prahlada felt liberated while remaining in his own body. He was easily able to break free of his shackles and rise to the surface of the water. In these ways, Prahlada always survived simply through the grace of God.

Holi celebrates one particular miracle relating to Prahlada's life. Hiranyakashipu had a sister named Holika, who had a special power that granted her immunity from the effects of fire. Hiranyakashipu thought this presented a great opportunity to finally be able to kill Prahlada. He decided to send Holika into a blazing fire while holding Prahlada in her lap. The result would be predictable enough: Holika would survive and Prahlada would die. Of course just the opposite happened. Prahlada kept his mind fixed on the lotus feet of Lord Vishnu, and instead it was Holika who was burned to ashes. This event has been celebrated ever since as Holi.

Prahlada Maharaja was a great devotee who authored a number of insightful prayers to Lord Vishnu, who appeared in front of him in His half-man/half-lion form of Narasimhadeva. We can learn a lot from this young child. He continues to be an object of worship to this day and a great authority on bhakti-yoga, or devotional service to Lord Krishna. We should remember God at all times, from our childhood all the way up until the time of death. God exists within us as the Supersoul and without as the spiritual master. These two things, working together, can deliver us perfection in life. Anyone who remembers Prahlada Maharaja and his teachings will surely attain eternal devotion to Lord Krishna.

HOLI II

rāma nāma nara kesarī kanakakasipu kalikāla |
jāpaka jana prahalāda jimi pālihi dali surasāla | |

"Shri Rama's holy name is like Narasimhadeva to the Hiranyakashipu-like Kali Yuga. For those who chant the holy name, the Lord offers them all protections and crushes their tormentors, just as He did for Prahlada Maharaja." (Dohavali, 26)

There was danger in the air. A sweet and innocent young child, who had no fault against him except a deep love and affection within his heart for his beloved Lord Vishnu, was about to be burned to death. Even in the strictest communities which employ the sternest of disciplinary measures, children are granted leniency for their transgressions. Should they break the law or fail to abide by the orders of the parents, punishment is rarely doled out, and if it is, it won't be very severe. But in this particular kingdom a long time ago the situation was reversed. The pious, kind and honorable were persecuted for understanding that man has limitations and that the true benefit of human life is to understand God and take to His loving service. Though sensing the impending doom, this young boy held firm in his vows. He simply remembered the holy name, the sound vibration representing His beloved savior, his life and soul, and he was subsequently saved from all dangers. Though the nature of the rescue seemed like a miracle of mythological proportions, this real-life, historical event of the boy's triumph over the forces of evil, a time when the holy name manifested in the form of a protective shield around a seemingly helpless soul who had no one else to save him, has been celebrated ever since as the occasion of Holi.

Holi is typically celebrated in a festive mood, with colors being thrown about in a playful manner. As with any other ancient tradition still honored today, it is understandable that the origins of the holiday would no longer be at the forefront of consciousness. In the Vedic tradition the annual festivals and celebrations typically focus on activities, pastimes and appearances of the Supreme

Personality of Godhead. Even in those individuals who aren't very religious, don't read many scriptural books, or fail to perform any outward worship, the general acknowledgement of a higher power is still usually present. The Vedas aim to arouse an even stronger spiritual sentiment out of every one of us by providing further information into the nature of the Supreme Being that we are all inclined to believe in and acknowledge. The more we get to know someone, especially an individual who possesses attractive features, the better the chances are that we'll develop an attachment to them and a desire to maintain a link with them for a longer period of time. Yoga is built on this foundation, as it represents a link in consciousness with the Supreme Lord, whose every aspect is ever-pure and all-pervading. Just as the radio waves emanating from a station can travel long distances, the sweet sounds glorifying Supreme Spirit can penetrate any and all areas. The key is to know which frequency to tune into to pick up the majestic sounds that please the heart and cause an arousal of the most intense and pure loving emotions man has ever known.

The annual celebration days help to organize and assemble masses of people in remembering and honoring the Lord. Though He is described by so many names in the multitudes of spiritual traditions around the world, His complete attractiveness forms His most important characteristic. For there to be an attraction that touches every individual and never dies, there must be a tangible form, one that is permanent. If God's form constantly changed, He wouldn't remain all-attractive. Since He is capable of luring in the kind-hearted souls in all the universes with His names, forms, pastimes and qualities, His most descriptive name is Krishna. Since He is capable of providing transcendental pleasure to others, He is also known as Rama. Since He is all pervading, in charge of the mode of goodness, and can be opulently adorned, He is also addressed as Vishnu. Indeed, the Vedas provide thousands of names for the original Divine Being, with each appellation capable of very effectively arousing the natural loving sentiments safely tucked away in the heart.

The key is to remember and honor these names regularly. Yet due to the influences of time and material nature, there are many layers covering up real knowledge and information about Supreme Spirit. Therefore the Vedic tradition puts forth holidays and celebrations as a way to regularly attack the thick wall of nescience enveloping the sincere souls deluded by the influences of the illusory energy of material nature, maya. Holi relates specifically to a five year old devotee named Prahlada. As the son of a king, he was groomed to be a great ruler, one adept in the political, diplomatic and military arts. Though kings are a rarity today, they were prominent in ages past. A good ruler is one who can govern with an iron fist and be able to withstand enemy attack at the same time. In this regard Hiranyakashipu, Prahlada's father, was very capable. He was so powerful that everyone in the world was afraid of him. Even the demigods, the saintly figures residing on the heavenly planets, were terrorized by him, so much so that they took on disguises to avoid being recognized by the demon king.

Prahlada was all set to follow in his father's footsteps, except for one small wrinkle. His mother had been instructed on the ancient art of bhakti, or devotional service, while she was pregnant with the boy. When Prahlada was born, he was able to remember everything Narada Muni, the celebrated devotee of Vishnu and tireless welfare worker, had spoken to his mother while he was in the womb. Therefore Prahlada wasn't attracted to material affairs in any way. When he was sent to school, he would listen to what the spiritual master taught him, but remain ever devoted to Vishnu all the while. Bhakti, or pure love, can only be directed at Vishnu or one of His non-different forms. The love that we are normally accustomed to feeling and acting upon is not counted as bhakti because of the defects in the sentiment and the object of worship. All the identified strong emotions of the material world, even hatred, are derived from the natural penchant for bhakti within the soul. When the loving sentiment is directed at the proper recipient, not only is the true potential for experiencing bliss achieved, but the love and affection felt for our fellow man also increases.

When Prahlada would come home from school, his father would ask him what he had learned. Obviously Hiranyakashipu was expecting to hear about how a king should use different methods such as divide-and-conquer, pacification, giving gifts, and punishment as ways of dealing with an enemy. But Prahlada told his father that he had learned that life's mission is bhakti-yoga, which can consist of hearing, chanting, remembering, worshiping, offering prayers, becoming a servant of the Lord, becoming His friend, carrying out His orders and surrendering everything unto Him. Hiranyakashipu didn't like hearing this at all. Due to his tremendous powers and his hatred of Vishnu, Hiranyakashipu thought that he was the Supreme Being. The Supreme Lord had previously killed Hiranyakashipu's brother Hiranyaksha. Therefore the demon was very envious of Vishnu and His authority. Now his son was glorifying vishnu-bhakti instead of describing how world domination could be had, so this was too much for the demon to take.

Hiranyakashipu first asked his son to stop worshiping and praising Vishnu, but when that didn't work, the demon tried to kill his five year old boy many times. Holi relates to the specific attempt that involved placing Prahlada in a pit of fire with a female demon named Holika. Her unique ability was to withstand any amount of fire that would normally consume anyone else. The plan was pretty straightforward. Holika would take Prahlada into a pit of fire and be able to survive herself, thereby removing the greatest source of distress for Hiranyakashipu. The demon was so hateful of the Supreme Lord that he couldn't even stand to hear the name of Vishnu, or Krishna. Of course the boy was just the opposite in behavior. He couldn't go very long without describing the Lord's glories. Prahlada tried to tell his father that Vishnu was his friend too, and that his tremendous abilities in fighting were due to Vishnu's grace.

Faced with impending death, Prahlada really didn't alter his behavior much. Just as he would normally do, he held on to the name of the Lord. Simply remembering His beloved Vishnu, Prahlada not only survived, but also caused Holika's abilities to backfire. Instead of Prahlada burning to death, it was Holika whom the fire consumed. The different colors of her ashes thus became the genesis of the tradition of throwing powdered colors around on Holi. It may seem strange to celebrate someone's ashes resulting from a gory death, but the memory of the incident with Prahlada is anything but unpleasant or ghoulish. Simply remembering the Lord's name and holding on to it with love and affection is enough to be protected from all calamities and impediments standing in the way of divine service.

Goswami Tulsidas, the revered poet and sweetheart of a person, especially loved chanting the name of Rama. Though Lord Rama is a historical personality and an incarnation of Godhead, Tulsidas never made the mistake of separating Rama from His other forms and activities. Indeed, Tulsidas very fondly remembered the protections offered by the Supreme Lord to Prahlada Maharaja. The incident with Holika was just one of many attempts made by Hiranyakashipu to kill his son. Yet, each and every time Prahlada followed the same procedure to escape danger. The Lord finally appeared on the scene in a manifested form, but this time not just to protect Prahlada. He instead came to do away with the boy's father. The name of God protected Prahlada at all times, and since the name is non-different from the Supreme Personality it represents, the Lord finally came to personally end Hiranyakashipu's reign of terror.

Though Krishna is considered the original form of Godhead, with Vishnu being a non-different expansion of the same, the form that came to kill Hiranyakashipu was quite unusual. It was seemingly a half man/half lion; hence He became known as Narasimhadeva. Hiranyakashipu had been previously granted many boons which afforded him protection from all sorts of attack. The Lord took into account all these conditions and crafted just the right form to kill Hiranyakashipu and simultaneously not break any of the promises given to him. The man-lion, Nara-kesari, came and did away with the tormenter of Prahlada once and for all. Though he felt sorry for his father, Prahlada did not protest. Indeed, he offered a flower garland to his beloved Vishnu while the whole event was transpiring.

Holi gives us a chance to remember the magnificent protections that come from the Lord's holy name and His divine appearances on earth in wonderfully brilliant forms like the half-man/half-lion. Tulsidas says that the Kali Yuga, the age we currently live in, can be likened to Hiranyakashipu. Just as the Daitya king was vehemently opposed to vishnu-bhakti, the makeup of society in today's age of quarrel and hypocrisy is such that devotional service goes primarily ignored. The dark influences of material nature have found a safe and protected home in the activities of meat eating, gambling, intoxication and illicit sex. Indeed, these sinful behaviors can only have a strong presence wherever there is an absence of real religion, the practice of divine love.

Just as Hiranyakashipu was incredibly strong, so the effects of Kali Yuga are difficult to overcome. But by remembering the name of the Lord, inimical influences in any form can be removed in an instant. Prahlada Maharaja witnessed this fact personally, so we can hold on to his example as proof of the claim. Those who regularly chant, "Hare Krishna Hare Krishna, Krishna Krishna, Hare Hare, Hare Rama Hare Rama, Rama Rama, Hare Hare", will surely be protected from all calamities and be allowed to swim in the ocean of transcendental bliss that is vishnu-bhakti.

HOLI III

When a person does extraordinary things, a mythology starts to build around them. The legend of so and so grows as each new person hears about their past exploits. Because of this tendency relating to the activities of ordinary human beings, the term "mythology" is sometimes invoked to downplay the behavior of past divine personalities. This is the resort of the less informed, whose judgment is clouded by the limits of personal perception. The event of Holi celebrates the ability of one particular person to defy the odds, and though what he did was extraordinary and seemingly miraculous, because of his internal qualities it was actually not surprising at all. In fact, similar feats have been repeated since time immemorial by those who are under the protection of the greatest protector.

The scene: a five year old boy awaiting a ride into a pit of fire. Think of going to an amusement park and getting strapped into a seat which is about to go places that you don't normally think to be safe. The thrill of the ride is based on the danger, the spinning around in circles of your body at violent speeds, all the while knowing that you probably won't get hurt. You are controlled in these situations; you are not in control. With this young child a long time ago, he was in the hands of an elder female, who was to take him into a pit of fire.

Oh, but this was no amusement park ride. As fire is not something you want to play around with, the elder woman had a trick up her sleeve. She thought she was immune to the effects of fire, and since the young boy was not, the desired result was her continuing to live and the boy dying. The order came from the boy's father of all people. Can we imagine such a thing? What could a young child do that would cause us to even contemplate doing something so horrible to them? Where must our mind be if we're willing to go through with such a dastardly act?

Actually, this father had previously made other vile attempts and would continue on afterwards. That's correct; the boy would survive the attack. Unfortunately for her and her boss, the elder woman would not. The effects reversed when the young boy was in her presence. You see the child, Prahlada Maharaja, was completely sinless. This doesn't mean that someone who is free of sin is automatically immune to the effects of fire, but in this particular circumstance the immunity relating to the fire transferred to the right person.

In the father's eyes, the child was a vile creature for having dedicated his life to worship of Lord Vishnu at such a young age. Vishnu is the qualified form of the Supreme Lord. He is the Personality of Godhead, opulently adorned and responsible for the creation and destruction of every universe. Vishnu is God, but with the features more defined than in the abstract vision. Vishnu is but an expansion of the original personality known as Krishna, who is all-attractive. Regardless of whether these statements are accepted or not, the key point is that devotion to the Supreme Lord, however you choose to see Him, is an innocent practice when followed under authorized guidelines.

If you deny God's existence, you will worship His external energy of material nature. There is harm with this route in the sense that matter is temporary, so whatever you choose to do will have only temporary effects. At the same time, others are performing the same worship, and since the external energy gives no protection, the competition leads to collisions and thus fosters the worst kinds of sentiments and emotions within people.

If you worship God as an impersonal energy or an abstract person from whom you ask things, your mode of worship is harmless in the sense that it's not directly hurting anyone else. You may be more prone to surrendering to the same material energy worshiped by the atheists, but there is still nothing wrong with at least thinking about God, knowing that He exists.

In bhakti-yoga, or devotional service, dedicated worship towards the real form of the Supreme Lord takes place. This style of worship is also known as Krishna consciousness, because the aim is to change the way that you think, to alter your thoughts to the point that you're always thinking about God. What could be the harm in this, especially if you're a youth? Why would Prahlada's father object so much?

The atheist takes shelter of material nature, and because of their denial of God's existence they essentially apply the "God" status to themselves. For all you know, nature does not have any intelligence. And you know that you are intelligent, so this means that you can control nature, as opposed to nature controlling you. Never mind the fact that you can't tell the sun when to rise and set and when the seasons to come and go, because you can get up at a certain time and speak when you want, you somehow think that you are God.

With Hiranyakashipu, the "I am God" mentality was strengthened by the fact that he had defeated all the powerful kings of the world. Even the celestials in the heavens were afraid of him. He had previously undergone great austerities to receive powers as benedictions, but once he received those strengths he forgot that he wasn't responsible for generating them.

The father wanted the son to follow in his footsteps, to rule the world with a strong hand. "What could be gained by worshiping Vishnu?", the father thought. To the atheist, God as a concept stands in the way of material enjoyment. He makes His worshipers suffer and needlessly renounce happiness in a temporary world. Of course, the devotee of Vishnu is knowledgeable, irrespective of the external conditions. Prahlada knew all about reincarnation, the temporary nature of material happiness, and the urgent need for following God consciousness in the precious human form of body. He was so intelligent that he kindly distributed this information to his classmates in school during recess.

Hiranyakashipu eventually became so sick of even hearing about Vishnu from Prahlada. The father decided that his son needed to die. One slight problem though. The boy was unbreakable. Nothing could kill him. The plot with Holika, Hiranyakashipu's sister, was one of the many schemes tried by the evil king. Though Holika had the boon to remain immune to fire, Prahlada survived the trip into the fire because Vishnu protects His devotees. He makes sure to give them conditions that are conducive to their cherished worship.

In fact, Vishnu gives the same protection to the atheists through the workings of maya, or illusion. The atheist is guaranteed to stay miserable in their surroundings, to have ample opportunities for eating, sleeping, mating and defending, which alone don't provide any satisfaction to the soul. There is no explicit protection from the Personality of Godhead in interactions with material nature, as the Lord is by default neutral, but at the same time the energy is non-different from the person who created it. Therefore the energy's dissipation of elements to be used in material enjoyment represents a sort of favor from the master.

The sinless Prahlada survived the trip into the fire, but Holika did not. The ashes from her body were of many different colors, and since that time the tradition has been to throw different colored powders in fun to celebrate the original event. Though a seemingly ghoulish way to celebrate an occasion, the colors of Holi represent the victory of Vishnu's devotee over the forces of evil. Prahlada thwarted all the attacks of Hiranyakashipu and did so without asking anything from the demigods. The celestials are powerful and act at the behest of Vishnu to grant benedictions, but at the same time Vishnu is the one who can give rewards to even them. This automatically makes Vishnu superior.

The devotee who loves Vishnu or one of His personal expansions like Lord Krishna or Lord Rama can receive the greatest favor. There needn't be any other master. And the attitude of service can continue in a mood of love, where the master eventually can't do anything to stop the devotee from offering service. Prahlada was sinless because he had no other desire than to chant the Lord's names and think of Him. No person, even a powerful king like Hiranyakashipu, can break the devotee's determination. Prahlada emerged victorious by remembering Vishnu's names, and so the wise souls of the Kali Yuga can escape the perils of material existence by regularly chanting, "Hare Krishna Hare Krishna, Krishna Krishna, Hare Hare, Hare Rama Hare Rama, Rama Rama, Hare Hare".

In Closing:

Prahlada Maharaja, devotion to Vishnu in him,
An innocent five year old, completely free of sin.

Boy's insistence on bhakti path father did not like,
Eventually wanted son out of his sight.

King's sister Holika immune to fire's pit,
In it brought Prahlada with him to sit.

Ah, but Vishnu's devotee from harm escaped,
To burn to ashes was instead Holika's fate.

Sinless son saved by saying Vishnu's names,
Tradition of Holi celebrates his fame.

RAMA NAVAMI I

"There was a king named Dasharatha, the protector of dharma, as unshakeable as a mountain, true to his promises, well known throughout the world, and whose son is Raghava. Raghava, who is known by the name of Rama, is a righteous soul, famous throughout the three worlds. He has long arms and wide eyes. He is my husband and worshipable deity." (Sita Devi speaking to Ravana, Valmiki Ramayana, Aranya Kand, 56.2-3)

Rama Navami celebrates the appearance of Lord Shri Ramachandra, an incarnation of God who descended to earth many thousands of years ago in Ayodhya, India. The holiday is named as such because of the specific day in the lunar cycle on which Lord Rama appeared. The Vedic calendar is based on the lunar cycle, with certain days being more auspicious than others. Lord Rama appeared on the ninth day of the waxing moon in the month of Chaitra, thus His birthday is celebrated as Rama Navami. It is similar to the concept of the Christmas Holiday where Christians celebrate the birthday of Lord Jesus Christ. Vedic holidays are a little different in that there are many Christmas-type celebrations each year since God takes unlimited forms, ananta rupam. Many of these forms appear on earth. God, being the original person, adi purusham, never actually takes birth, so His birthdays are more aptly referred to as appearances. Since the Lord descends from the spiritual world in an eternally existing form, His appearances are known as avataras. Lord Rama is one of God's primary avataras.

The circumstances surrounding His birth were interesting. During the Treta Yuga, the second time period of creation, there was a great king ruling over the earth by the name of Dasharatha. He only ruled over the town of Ayodhya, but since his dominion was recognized by all the other kings, he was often referred to as mahipati, or the Lord of the earth. Dasharatha's trademark characteristic was his chivalry and kindness. He was famous throughout the world as a great warrior who was dedicated to dharma. The Vedas tell us that an ideal government is one run by the warrior class of men, the kshatriyas. This is because a government's primary duty is to provide protection to the innocent.

Therefore a king, or government leader, must exhibit great fighting skills and strength in order to instill fear in the hearts of the miscreants. If the sinful among us understand that they will suffer the consequences should they harass the innocent, society will function much more peacefully. Thus Dasharatha, through his great fighting ability demonstrated in countless wars, established his supremacy throughout the world.

Dasharatha pretty much had it all. He was wholly dedicated to dharma, or his occupational duty. Dharma actually means "that which constantly exists with the particular object". Thus dharma is that which sustains one's existence. Since the living entity's existence is defined by its relationship with God, dharma usually refers to religiosity or religious duty. When applied to specific areas, such as government, it refers to the code of conduct or righteousness. Dasharatha's citizens were very happy, and he personally enjoyed life with his three wives. The Vedas tell us that those in the mode of passion, the warrior class, are allowed to marry more than once provided that they can guarantee the complete protection of their wives. The tongue and the genitals are two of the hardest organs to control, so they represent the two biggest stumbling blocks towards advancing in spiritual life. All the Vedic guidelines are put in place so as to help the living entity achieve pure Krishna, or God, consciousness in their lifetime. Only with this mindset can the soul break free of the perpetual cycle of birth and death. We shouldn't mistakenly think that the Vedas and the gurus who follow them are unnecessarily punishing us with their rules and regulations. The complete set of Vedic guidelines represents a form of tough love. Since sex desire is very difficult to control, it is advised that one get married at a very young age, and then only indulge in sex life for the purpose of having children.

From this injunction, we can logically conclude that sex life can only be allowed during one period in every month, when the wife is fertile. The warrior class lives mostly in the mode of passion, meaning they perform work for the purpose of receiving material gain. An outgrowth of living in the mode of passion is that one's sex desires remain very high. To allow kings to indulge in sex life but still remain committed to dharma, they were allowed to keep more than one wife. This way the women of society were still protected, and the kings could still make spiritual progress.

Dasharatha had one thing that bothered him though. He had no son to whom he could pass on his kingdom. The Vedas tell us that each person acquires three debts at the time of birth. One of these debts is to the forefathers, also known as the pitrs. This logically makes sense because if it weren't for our parents, we would not take birth under the circumstances that we do. The father must work very hard to maintain the family and the mother goes through so much pain during labor. Thus there is a natural feeling of obligation to repay the sacrifices made by our parents. This debt actually ascends all the way up the family chain since our grandparents and forefathers also played an important role in determining the circumstances of our birth. The debt to the pitrs can be paid by begetting a son. For Dasharatha, this debt was increased due to the fact that he was a king in a very famous dynasty known as the Ikshvakus.

The Bible says that God created everything in the beginning. The Vedas give a similar description of the events at the time of creation, including the names of important personalities. The kings are known as rajarishis in the Vedic tradition because they are meant to act as God's representatives on earth. No one can protect better than God, so He decided that societies on earth would need one of His representatives to provide a similar level of protection on a micro scale. To this end, two lines of famous kings were started at the beginning of creation. One line took birth from the moon-god, Soma, and the other from the sun-god, Vivasvan. The Ikshvakus were part of the solar dynasty, and they were famous throughout the world. If Dasharatha didn't beget a son, he would be doing a great disservice to the family name.

In order to remedy the situation, the king was advised to hold a grand sacrifice. These events took place in the Treta Yuga, or second time period of creation. The Vedas tell us that for each of the four ages of creation, there is a specific method of worship that is most effective in providing transcendental realization. In the first age, the recommended method was deep meditation. Almost everyone lived in rural areas, thus there were few distractions. Many yogis lived in forests known as tapo-vanas, meaning forests suitable for the performance of austerities. In the Treta Yuga, the recommended method was elaborate sacrifice. Today, Vedic sacrifices are celebrated on a small scale, with a small fire and some oblations of ghee poured into it. In the Treta Yuga, these sacrifices were very elaborate and required highly qualified brahmanas to perform.

Dasharatha performed the Ashvamedha sacrifice, and a subsequent Putrakameshti yajna, as was recommended to him. A great deity came out of the sacrificial altar and handed some payasam to Dasharatha. He in turn divided the payasam up and distributed it to his three wives. Very quickly they all became pregnant, with Queen Kausalya eventually giving birth to Lord Rama. Dasharatha's two other wives, Kaikeyi and Sumitra, gave birth to Bharata, Lakshmana, and Shatrughna. Thus the king was blessed with four beautiful sons, but Rama remained his favorite. Lord Rama was Dasharatha's prananatha, or the lord of his life air.

Rama was the son that Dasharatha had longed for. Like father like son, Rama too was extremely dedicated to dharma. Never did He speak an ill word to Dasharatha, for He loved His father very much. The driving force behind Rama's activities was His dedication to maintaining the good name of His father. Rama viewed Dasharatha as His foremost deity, setting a great example for future generations to follow.

God didn't appear only to give Dasharatha a son. At the time, there was a powerful Rakshasa demon by the name of Ravana who was terrorizing the saintly class of men around the world. Ravana was very strong due to boons he had secured from several demigods, thus everyone was afraid to take him on in battle. It was at the behest of the demigods that God decided to appear as Lord Rama. Due to the boons he received, Ravana was guaranteed protection in battle against all types of creatures, including celestials. The only species that could defeat him were the human beings. Thus Lord Rama, appearing in the guise of an ordinary human being, was prophesized to be the destroyer of Ravana.

Since Ravana hadn't directly attacked Ayodhya, there was no way for Rama to go after him and still remain on the virtuous path. Being God Himself, Rama could have easily done whatever He wanted to, but at the same time, He wanted to set a good example for how a king should behave. To secure Ravana's demise, the demigods set forth a plan whereby Lord Rama would have an excuse to take him on in battle. The first piece of this puzzle was Rama's exile to the forest. Dasharatha wanted Rama to succeed him on the throne, but plans got changed at the last minute due to a fit of jealousy thrown by Kaikeyi. She requested that Bharata become king and Rama be exiled. Dasharatha couldn't ignore these requests because he had granted her any two boons of her choosing on a previous occasion.

For His part, Lord Rama didn't want His father to turn out to be a liar, so He gladly accepted the exile punishment. Rama's beautiful and chaste wife, Sita Devi, insisted on accompanying Him, as did Lakshmana. While they were in the forest, Sita was kidnapped by Ravana after a diversion was set up whereby both Rama and Lakshmana were drawn away from the group's cottage. The demigods were quite pleased by this, for they knew that Ravana had met his end. Lord Rama and Lakshmana eventually marched to Lanka, with the help of a huge band of monkeys, and defeated Ravana in battle. Sita was rescued and the group triumphantly returned to Ayodhya, where Rama was crowned as the king.

The beauty of Rama Navami is that it not only celebrates Lord Rama, but all of His devotees as well. In pictures, Lord Rama is usually seen standing alongside Sita and Lakshmana, with Hanumanji offering his obeisances in front of them. Hanuman was part of the Vanara army, and played an integral role in Sita's rescue and Ravana's defeat. God is never alone, for His closest associates always remain with Him. This is the view of God given to us by the Vedas. God is the energetic and the devotees are His energy. The two are meant to always be together, side-by-side, enjoying eternal felicity.

Lord Rama is God Himself, so it's hard to accurately put His qualities into words. Therefore we must study the qualities of His close associates to get an idea. They say that you can judge a person's character by the company they keep, and in Lord Rama's case, we see that He had the best friends in the world. Sita, Hanuman, and Lakshmana are so exalted that it is virtually impossible to find a person who can say anything negative about them. Hanumanji is so great that there is an entire book, the Sundara-kanda, in the famous Ramayana poem dedicated to his exploits. Sita and Lakshmana always identified themselves as servants of Rama, and they never ran out of praiseworthy things to say about the Lord.

As spirit souls, part and parcel of God, we are meant to be His energy; we are meant to please Him in the same way that Sita, Hanuman, and Lakshmana do. Celebrating festivals like Rama Navami and Janmashtami are great ways to get into the spiritual mindset. Taking it one step further, we should all try to remember God and His devotees every single day of the year. This can easily be accomplished by regularly chanting, "Hare Krishna Hare Krishna, Krishna Krishna, Hare Hare, Hare Rama Hare Rama, Rama Rama, Hare Hare".

RAMA NAVAMI II

āju sudina subha gharī suhā'ī |
rūpa-sīla-guna-dhāma rāma nṛpa-bhavana praga|ta bhae ā'ī | |

"Today is the most auspicious day; the time and circumstance are joyous and beautiful. Shri Rama, the abode of beauty, character and divine qualities, has appeared in the king's palace." (Gitavali, 1.1.1)

Shri Rama Navami, the appearance day anniversary of the compassionate Lord, the abode of all virtue and good qualities, Shri Ramachandra, the jewel of the Raghu dynasty, the only savior for those who have abandoned all hope for finding satisfaction in a temporary world full of ups and downs, defeats and gains and losses and victories, is especially honored, remembered and celebrated by the devotees. While worshiping God and dedicating our lives to His service entails a daily dedication to action and routine, the holidays of the Vedic tradition, the special occasions that bring an added emphasis on remembrance, help to both maintain the devotional mindset and also bring others into the celebration, allowing everyone in the world to feel the transcendental bliss that can only come through mental association with our dearmost friend, the living being who never undergoes birth or death and who remains steadfast in His vow to always protect the surrendered souls.

More than a mere process of religion or spirituality, complete and total surrender to God enacted voluntarily in a mood of love and affection represents the true dharma of the soul, the constitutional mindset for every form of life. Yet only in the human species can the distinctions between lifestyles and activities even be made. This assessment will ideally be followed by a sober evaluation, where tasks are properly prioritized. Of all the priorities we may think take precedence, none is more important than the maintaining of the fidelity of the relationship with the Supreme Spirit, the spiritual entity who resides within our heart next to the individual soul. For all of eternity, it's just the two of us, ourselves and the Supreme Lord, who never leaves us for even a second.

Does this mean that God is with us right now? The Supreme Person's presence can be felt during every second of every day within every sphere of life. But only through an advanced level of intelligence, one secured through rigorous training following humble submission to a bona fide spiritual master, an authority figure who has himself abandoned all other engagements in life that have no relation to bhakti, or divine love, can this omnipresence of the Supreme Lord and His accompanying worthiness of worship be properly understood. At the time of birth, these concepts remain unknown to us, especially if our accepted body type happens to be a lower form, like that of an animal. If it eats, sleeps, mates and defends, it's a form of life. If the autonomous entity goes through birth, old age, disease and death, it is a life. Never mind its level of intelligence or whether or not it knows who or what God is. Indeed, many human beings take to stupid activity, reckless and nonsensical behavior that doesn't further any tangible purpose. Despite the presence of such fools, we would never consider them to not be living beings, to not have souls inside of them. Similarly, even the animal kingdom, though not having anywhere near the intelligence levels of human beings, are God's children, spirit souls who have every right to be in the association of the Supreme Lord.

Through bhakti the divine consciousness can be awakened. Knowledge of God and His spiritual attributes is currently resting in a dormant state within the heart, like a book that hasn't been opened for a very long time. Just like their Supreme Father, every living being is eternally blissful and knowledgeable, but since God is superior, only He can retain these properties at the highest levels at all times. The individual spirit souls, when choosing to leave the personal company of the Ultimate Reservoir of Pleasure, have their attributes deprecated by both the natural effects of material nature and the competing forces vying for supremacy. A fire can burn at a great intensity provided it has enough fuel and objects to consume. The living entities have potencies that function similarly, but in the conditioned state their abilities are limited to the body type they accept. In the spiritual land, however, where everyone wants to serve the Lord, there are no limitations on action or enjoyment. Therefore through a simple shift in consciousness, wherein thoughts and desires are turned towards meeting the interests of the Supreme Lord, from whom all our wonderful qualities emanate, the supreme destination can be attained. With that return to the spiritual realm, the primary source of all miseries in life gets removed, thereby allowing the soul to enjoy a permanent blissful condition.

Sharanagati is the process of full and complete surrender that brings about this bliss. Realizing the need for surrender is quite difficult, especially if we have been programmed otherwise through many lifetimes on earth. Therefore explicit processes of bhakti are required to help train the mind properly. The most effective method of devotional service for the people of the present age is the chanting of the holy names, "Hare Krishna Hare Krishna, Krishna Krishna, Hare Hare, Hare Rama Hare Rama, Rama Rama, Hare Hare". The word "Krishna" describes the Supreme Lord's form as the all-attractive wielder of the flute and the delight of the residents of Vrajabhumi, the spiritual land of Vrindavana. Rama addresses the jewel of the Raghu dynasty, the pious and handsome prince who appeared in the family of King Dasharatha on the wonderful occasion of Rama Navami. The key benefit of chanting the names of God is that time is spent engaged in devotional service, and thus consciousness can get shifted.

All processes of bhakti-yoga have the same objective, that of keeping the thoughts of the mind focused on the Supreme Lord, His names, activities and pastimes. As consciousness is the key ingredient in attaining spiritual salvation, it would make sense that remembering, or smaranam, would be another important tool employed by the sincere transcendentalist following the bhakti tradition. Indeed, remembering alone can solve all problems, as the mind can travel millions of miles to another land, and even many years into the past. Goswami Tulsidas, the celebrated Vaishnava poet, in his Gitavali seemingly travels directly back into time with his spiritually infused mind to delight in the occasion of Rama's appearance in Ayodhya, an event which occurred many thousands of years ago during the Treta Yuga.

In the above quoted verse, Tulsidas is declaring the day of Rama's appearance to be all-auspicious. Having mentally transferred himself to the city of Ayodhya on the wonderful day of Rama's advent, the poet notes that during this time all external conditions are favorable and conducive towards good fortune. Though according to our estimation Rama was a historical personality who appeared on this earth in the past, the comings and goings of the Supreme Lord and His various incarnations constantly take place in other universes as well. Therefore remembering God and His pastimes doesn't necessarily have to involve focusing on the past. Somewhere at this very minute Shri Rama is appearing on an earthly planet, and His beloved devotee Tulsidas is gladly watching the scene and noting the behavior of the wonderful citizens of Ayodhya-dhama.

Shri Rama appeared in a royal dynasty, one descending from the first king on earth, Maharaja Ikshvaku. Due to the family's exalted status, whenever a son was born into their line, it was a big deal. At the time of Rama's advent, the present ruler of the dynasty, Maharaja Dasharatha, was without a son. Therefore the birth of the first son from the womb of Queen Kaushalya, the king's wife, was a grand occasion, one that signaled the beginning of the transfer of ownership of the kingdom to a new generation. But this was no ordinary son. As the Supreme Lord, Rama is the abode of all good qualities, character and beauty. It is a mistaken belief by some transcendentalists that the material world is false and thus the cause of only misery. Any object, without knowing how to make proper use of it, can certainly be damaging. And it is indeed a fact that the material universe was created to facilitate the desires of those souls who wanted to imitate God in the areas of creation, maintenance and destruction. In the material land, the pure spirit souls are enveloped by gunas, or material qualities, which can be of the goodness, passion or ignorance variety.

But gunas can immediately become spiritualized if they are used to further one's God consciousness. Since matter comes from God, when it is associated with Him, it becomes glorious and completely spiritual. Indeed, the spiritual world is not filled with void or formlessness. There is to be found every variety of engagement and beauty within the transcendental sphere. Distinctions are made between the two lands because matter in the imperishable realm is considered divine, or daivi prakriti. Shri Rama is the origin of all gunas, or the abode of all qualities. Wherever He goes, all His transcendental traits come with Him.

Rama is also the most beautiful, as that is one of the features possessed by Bhagavan, or the Supreme Personality of Godhead who is replete with the six opulences of beauty, wealth, strength, fame, wisdom and renunciation simultaneously. Just one look at the smiling face of Shri Ramachandra is enough to defeat the pride of even the staunchest devotee of gross matter. Rama is also of the highest character, both under the spiritual estimation and also under the regulative principles of piety. In reality, religious principles, or the most important law codes, only exist to allow one to eventually understand the Supreme Person and His worthiness of worship. But Rama, as a ruler of a pious group of citizens, made sure to uphold the dedication to dharma so nicely passed down to Him from the previous members of the Ikshvaku dynasty.

Since Rama is the abode of every wonderful quality, it is to be understood that He is never bereft of anything. The devotees who associate with Him get to bask in these transcendental features and realize the true benefit to having an existence. In all other spheres of life, we are attracted by wonderful qualities such as beauty and character. These features factor in how we form our friendships and decide on which engagements to take up. Since the Supreme Lord is the storehouse of all energy, material and spiritual, anyone who loves Him with all their heart will have no need to turn towards any other activity, as the attractiveness of Rama is enough to maintain the steady link in consciousness to the transcendental world that is yoga.

Rama's appearance took place in the Vedic month of Chaitra, which is based on the lunar calendar. Because He appeared on the ninth day of the moon cycle, His appearance celebration is known as Rama Navami. All signs were auspicious on this day, as the exact constellation of stars at a particular time can forebode evil or great fortune. Not surprisingly, Rama descended to earth at a time where everything was auspicious. All the creatures in Ayodhya, both animate and inanimate, were thrilled, for they were about to gain the direct audience of the Supreme Lord. The brahmanas of the community, those of the priestly order, were also ecstatic, so they started to chant the glories of the Lord as a way to welcome His appearance. Just as an exalted guest is welcomed with well-wishing words and sumptuous food, the residents of Ayodhya made sure that Rama knew that they were thrilled to see Him.

The celestials, the demigods managing the material affairs, were on the scene playing songs and dropping flowers from the sky. Mother Kaushalya was especially thrilled, for her first son was about to be born. Through Him she would gain eternal fame, as she would go on to be respected as the most wonderful mother, a sweetheart of a lady who never deviated in thought, word or deed from her vow to love Shri Rama. Tulsidas says that the happiness felt by everyone on that first Rama Navami was too great for him to even describe.

Though Maharaja Dasharatha was very excited to have his first son, he nevertheless made sure to abide by all the regulative principles, calling in the priests to perform the perfunctory rituals and regulations. Dasharatha purified himself in every way, as the opportunity to witness the appearance of the Supreme Lord in the form of a small child represents the most wonderful benediction. Just as we bathe in the morning and prepare ourselves nicely before going out in public, the emphasis on purity is enhanced when one is about to see Shri Rama face-to-face.

The royal palace was filled with singing and glorification of the Supreme Lord. In the Vedic tradition auspicious occasions are typically celebrated by giving charity to others. As the mission of human life is to understand God and the need for worshiping Him, every prescribed regulation is aimed at minimizing the effects of the senses and the possessive mentality assumed at the time of birth. Giving in charity is a great form of sacrifice, a way to loosen attachment to possessions which originally belong to God. On this occasion the primary wealth that was distributed was the sweet singing of the devotees and their constant attention on the holy name.

Outside the palace, everything was wonderfully decorated, with opulence and extravagance visible everywhere. At the palace gates, bards, their disciples and well-wishers were all present singing the praises of Shri Rama before He even appeared. The women of the city decked themselves out very nicely and arrived in throngs at the front of the palace, bringing with them all sorts of gifts for the new child, hoping for His long and prosperous life. Under a government not driven by God consciousness, the citizens are always leery of sending money to the state, for taxes are considered the greatest burden. But in the wonderful kingdom presided over by Maharaja Dasharatha, the women, the maintainers of the family, were enthusiastic to celebrate the wonderful occasion of Rama's birth and bring Him the most wonderful gifts as a sign of their appreciation.

The roads were so filled with sprinkled liquid preparations, such as saffron and water mixtures, that there was a slush created. But everyone was so jubilant in their dancing that they didn't notice anything around them. They had transcended the effects of their material bodies through transcendental ecstasy borne of anticipation of the appearance of Shri Rama. Only in bhakti can something as innocent and simple as dancing be a source of supreme felicity, providing a benefit greater than that found through meditational yoga, study of the scriptures, or any other engagement.

Maharaja Dasharatha gave away many cows, horses, elephants, jewels and gold in charity to the proper recipients. This was the happiest day in his life, so he was going to share his joy with others. It is said that all the siddhis, or perfections in life, could be found in his palace, as there can be no perfection greater than having the Supreme Lord visit your home and be welcomed in such a wonderful way by so many people.

Tulsidas says that the saints, demigods and brahmanas were all delighted at this time, while the miscreants were very unhappy. This foretells of future events, as Rama would go on to destroy the most powerful enemy forces terrorizing the innocent people of the world. The saintly class of men, the suras, are always delighted just to even think of Shri Rama, while the demons are always trying to undercut His authority and His Supreme Position. During even the most auspicious occasion of Rama's birth, the demons could find no joy.

A small drop of the Supreme Lord's limitless transcendental energy has empowered wonderful figures like Lord Brahma and Lord Shiva with divine abilities and tremendous fame, but the same energy was in such great abundance in Ayodhya on Rama Navami that it was flooding the entire city. This comparison by Tulsidas points to Lord Vishnu's supreme position as the origin of all life and the worshipable figure of even great personalities like Shiva and Brahma. Though they are divine entities in charge of the material modes of passion and ignorance, they sometimes must break their concentration and their focus on the lotus feet of the Supreme Lord. The residents of Ayodhya, however, were fully swooning with transcendental ecstasy, for the very same Vishnu was coming to grant them His darshana. This comparison also indicates that Shri Rama is a non-different form of the original Personality, so He is not lacking anything in terms of features. Energy expansions, or transcendental sparks, emanating from Vishnu create the innumerable living entities and also give them their power. But the origin of all energy, the reservoir of pleasure Himself, had personally descended to Ayodhya.

Tulsidas says that the evidence of the wonderful results that come from remembering the Lord was seen that day in Ayodhya. God consciousness secured through the bhakti mindset is a force like no other. Through remembering the divine appearance of Shri Rama and the wonderful activities He would go on to perform in the company of His dear associates like Sita Devi, Lakshmana and Hanuman, we can get a taste of what the residents of Ayodhya felt on that wonderful day, the time the Lord of their life came to rescue them from the doldrums of material existence. May the same level of devotion found in them awaken in our hearts, and may we never forget such a wonderful and benevolent master as Shri Rama.

RAMA NAVAMI III

subhaga seja sobhita kausilyā rucira rāma-sisu goda liye |
bāra-bāra bidhubadana bilokati locana cāru cakora kiye | |

"The most fortunate Kausalya looks charming as she sits on the beautiful bedstead holding the child Rama in her lap. Gazing upon His moon-like face again and again, she makes her eyes like a Chakora bird to His form." (Gitavali, 7.1)

Rama Navami celebrates the appearance day of Lord Ramachandra, the delight of the Raghu dynasty, who has a moon-like countenance to please the Chakora-like devotees, who never tire of gazing upon His beautiful face, which wears an enchanting smile and gives off a soothing radiance that douses the fire of material suffering. In fact, it is the association with the divine that is the only remedy for all ills, for the root of pain and misery is forgetfulness of that supremely fortunate person, who holds every opulence at the same time and to the fullest degree; hence one of His many names is Bhagavan.

In general social etiquette, it is not polite to stare at others. The reason for this should be quite obvious. Would you like it if someone else was looking at you all the time? Perhaps you wouldn't mind the attention if the sentiment was positive, but after a while, the instinctual reaction would be, "Hey man, quit looking at me! Can I help you with something?" Indeed, the gawking husband has been the painful burden of the devoted wife for ages, as the man can't help but try to assess the attractiveness of another female when he first sees her. Of course this is very rude behavior towards the wife, for the desire to look at another woman indicates that the man might not be pleased with whom he has for a life partner.

One sneaky way to get around the impoliteness of staring is to find situations where the person being looked at either doesn't know what you are doing or is powerless to stop you. Thankfully for us, the creator made one situation which is favorable for staring and which also doesn't violate any common standards of decency. The young child, especially the dependent, can be looked at nonstop, especially if they are really new to this world. Their vision can be so enchanting, making you really believe in a higher power, for how else to explain such innocence placed into a tiny bundle of joy? For a mother a long time ago, she couldn't help but stare at her newborn. To make the situation that much more auspicious, the delight she held in her lap was the honoree of the soon-to-be instituted tradition of Rama Navami.

During a period of time in the Treta Yuga, King Dasharatha was at the helm of Raghu's clan, the dynasty of kings originating with King Ikshvaku and which subsequently had the good fortune of including King Raghu as one of its members. The descendants in that line were thus often referred to as Raghava. A key for rulers in this family was to keep it going. If you have a famous family that is known for its ability to protect the citizens, to give them proper guidance in all matters of life and to keep out the influence of sin and vice, including that which comes from foreign attack, it's important to keep that line of succession going. This way the citizens won't have to worry when the king gets old. They can rest assured knowing that he will pass on his good reputation and character to his heir.

This was the problem for Dasharatha. He had no sons to whom to pass down the kingdom. After consulting with his royal priests, it was decided that a sacrifice would be held. The queens would eat the remnants of that sacrifice, and from that sanctified food they would become pregnant with child. Sure enough, everything went according to plan, except no one could predict the beauty and grace of the four children. The four sons born to Dasharatha were expansions of Lord Vishnu, the Supreme Personality of Godhead in His opulently adorned, four-handed form.

The eldest Rama was Vishnu Himself, and the three younger brothers were partial expansions. Queen Kausalya gave birth to Rama, Kaikeyi to Bharata, and Sumitra to Lakshmana and Shatrughna. The children were a delight for their mothers, and Rama was especially enchanting to everyone, including Dasharatha.

There is much attention paid when a new child is born, and since these boys were to be successors in the ancestral line, there was even more celebration when they took birth.

Brahmanas were fed, cows were milked, and gifts were distributed quite liberally by the king. The townspeople felt as if the four boys were their own children, so they showed up to the royal palace with so many gifts. They also decorated their homes very nicely, creating auspiciousness all around. Whenever the Supreme Lord personally appears, there is automatically an auspicious condition, but these residents had pure love, so they didn't take anything for granted. They prayed for the welfare of the four sons, that they would grow up to be brave, strong, pious, and just as dedicated to the welfare of all as Dasharatha.

Queen Kausalya had a special benefit, for she got to spend time with Rama alone. In those quiet moments, she got to stare at her young child, and there was nothing He could do about it. As one gets a little older, the smothering attention from the mother can become a bother. The child doesn't know any better, as they can't understand at such a young age what type of attachment the mother has formed with them. In the infant years, though, the child can only pleasantly smile in return when the mother constantly stares at them.

In the above referenced verse from the Gitavali of Goswami Tulsidas, we see that Dasharatha's chief queen looked especially charming when seated on her wonderful bedstead. She held the Supreme Lord in her lap, for she earned His company from pious acts performed in previous lives. Can we imagine the happiness she felt? The most beautiful person in the world lay in her lap in a form that required motherly affection. He was in front of her in a special form that best brought out spontaneous, parental affection, loving feelings that were not inhibited in any way.

Of course to try to understand Kausalya's feelings at the time is a little difficult, so the kind poet gives us some help. He says that she made her eyes like those of the Chakora bird, which constantly stares at the moon. The Chakora has a pure love for the moon, for it looks constantly at the bright luminous body in the dark sky and doesn't ask for anything in return. No other light gives it as much happiness, and when that moon is gone, there is no source of happiness that can replace it.

In a similar manner, Queen Kausalya's only source of pleasure was Rama, and because of this she was considered most fortunate, or subhaga. How can she be described in any other way? Where we get our primary pleasure is what will determine how fortunate or unfortunate we are. The drunkard worships the bottle of whiskey and thus finds only distress amidst illusory and temporary elation. The gambler worships the game and the next roll of the dice, and the sensually stirred person hangs on the next move of their significant other, not realizing that the same type of pleasure is already available to the less intelligent animals. The voracious meat eater takes their pleasure from the flesh of animals that were needlessly killed.

Because these sources are not pure, those taking their primary pleasure from them will be in unfortunate circumstances. On the other hand, one who finds pleasure from the person who is the most fortunate, Bhagavan, can in many ways be considered more fortunate than God Himself. Lord Rama has the company of His devotees and His pleasure potency expansions like Sita Devi, but the Chakora-like devotees have the association of both Shri Rama and His associates. As they depend only upon Rama and His every move for their happiness, they are never bereft of the pleasure that is every person's birthright.

On Rama Navami, we celebrate that very fortunate queen, who would love her son for the rest of her life. He would have to leave her company several times when He got older, but never did He leave her heart. She constantly gazed upon His moon-like face, and not at any time was the behavior impolite. On the contrary, the Chakora-like devotees know that devotion is the only auspicious path, and that through following it Rama will never abandon them, either in this life or the next.

In Closing:

In common circumstances impolite to stare,
To look at someone for too long we don't dare.

In one situation that behavior is actually fine,
To stare at newborn, they are too young to mind.

Shri Rama created this for His loving mother,
She stared at Him in her quiet room, for God no bother.

So adorable was the Supreme Lord in the small size,
That mother like a Chakora bird made her eyes.

On Rama Navami the mother and son we celebrate,
To Lord and devotee's pleasure this life we dedicate.

NARASIMHA CHATURDASHI I

There is one cause which is responsible for all causes. Each of us has a vital force inside us, but there is one vital force that is the source of all energy. This single dominating force is known as ishvara parama, or the Supreme Controller, and everything rests upon Him. Just as the laws of gravity operate on all objects without any prejudice, this dominating force applies to every living entity. Though most of us refer to this supreme divine entity as God, the Vedas give us much more descriptive names for the Supreme Absolute Truth. This Supreme Lord, who possesses innumerable transcendental qualities, kindly appears in front of our eyes from time to time in various shapes. One such famous appearance occurred many millions of years ago. Narasimha-chaturdashi marks the anniversary of when God came to earth in the form of a half-man/half-lion to kill the demon Hiranyakashipu. Since God's form was a mixture of a lion (simha) and a man (nara), this specific avatara is known as Narasimhadeva, and He holds a special place in the hearts of devotees around the world.

When the Lord comes to earth to enact pastimes, it is a significant occasion. This is because God doesn't choose to personally appear before us all the time. Most of the good and bad results of our actions are distributed by the demigods, elevated living entities who are given extraordinary powers by God Himself. Karma relates to fruitive activity, or any action taken which further develops the material body, or the outer covering of the soul. In this regard, nothing can really be good or bad as it relates to karma. We may take something to be beneficial to us, but to someone else, the same result can be deemed harmful. Thus the Supreme Lord doesn't take a personal interest in karma-phalam, or the results of fruitive activity.

Most of us can understand how karma works. You perform a good deed and you will be duly rewarded. You perform a sinful act and you will be punished in the future. It's interesting to see just how these results manifest. For example, the severity of the negative consequences that come about is commensurate with the severity of the crime committed. Though most followers of the Vedic tradition are vegetarians, there are still some who engage in meat eating. For such people, who are in the mode of ignorance, the Vedas provide a system whereby meat eating is sanctioned with the hopes of allowing the ignorant to further progress in spiritual understanding. When an animal is killed in one of these sanctioned sacrifices, the mantra recited within the ear of the animal goes something like this, "I'm killing you now so that I can eat your meat. You now have sanction to kill me in the same manner in a future life." Hence, we see the concept of an eye for an eye. What goes around comes around.

For extraordinary cases, God Himself intervenes. These cases don't involve karma, for as we already mentioned, the demigods take care of distributing the results of fruitive activity. What other type of work is there? Since karma relates to actions which lead to the development of the material body, there is another higher discipline which leads to the development of the spiritual body. The soul is pure, unchangeable, and unbreakable, thus it can never really develop. It can evolve, however, in the sense of where it chooses to reside. We are currently in a conditioned state, meaning our soul is covered by a material dress. This dress is composed of matter, an inferior energy, and thus it constantly goes through changes. We can get a spiritual body, though, if we choose to. In order to develop a permanent spiritual body, we must take up a discipline which is above karma.

Bhakti yoga, or the linking of the soul with God through works of love and devotion, is commonly referred to as devotional service. How does this activity differ from karma? On the surface, the specific actions may not look all that different, but the mindset of the performer is where the discrepancy lies. For example, we may walk around all day singing our favorite songs in our head, but the purpose of this activity is to provide pleasure to our mind and senses. Another person can be singing, "Hare Krishna Hare Krishna, Krishna Krishna, Hare Hare, Hare Rama Hare Rama, Rama Rama, Hare Hare", and have a completely different mindset. Krishna is the original name for God, the same God that all of us worship. Rama is also one of His names, and Hare refers to His energy in the form of His pleasure potency expansions. Thus chanting Hare Krishna is our way of asking God to always allow us to serve Him in an uninterrupted and unmotivated manner. Hence we see there is a gulf of difference between ordinary singing and singing God's names.

Devotional service actually consists of nine distinct processes, which have been outlined by the great devotee Prahlada Maharaja. Many many moons ago, there was a devotee born in a family of demons. The Vedas give us the lineage of the first few generations of mankind and also of other important species. There was a race of demons known as Daityas, so named because they were born from a woman named Diti. The Daityas inherited demonic qualities at the time of birth, and thus they were enemies of the devotees. Prahlada Maharaja, though taking birth as the son of a Daitya, had the qualities of a devotee. At the time, a great demon by the name of Hiranyakashipu, the eldest son of Diti, was terrorizing the world. He was well acquainted with the principles of dharma, artha, and kama. Yet he was still a demon, meaning he only wanted religiosity, economic development, and sense gratification for his own pleasure. This shows that there are varying degrees of dharma, or religiosity, and that not all dharmas are the same.

Prahlada, though a son of Hiranyakashipu, was a devotee of Lord Krishna from the time of his birth. This is because while he was still in the womb of his mother, Prahlada heard spiritual topics relating to Lord Krishna from the venerable Narada Muni. Thus the boy, though genetically predisposed to demoniac qualities, was born a devotee. As any good father would do, Hiranyakashipu sent his son Prahlada to school to get a good education. Hiranyakashipu was a king, so naturally he wanted Prahlada to succeed him on the throne one day. In order to be a good king, one must be well educated on matters pertaining to politics, religion, diplomacy, war, and economics. Prahlada, however, had no interest in these topics. He listened attentively to his teachers, but the boy still kept his mind always fixed on the lotus feet of the Supreme Lord.

One day when Prahlada came home from school, Hiranyakashipu affectionately took him on his lap and asked his beloved son what he had learned. To his surprise, Hiranyakashipu heard all about the greatness of Lord Vishnu from Prahlada. Hiranyakashipu viewed Lord Vishnu, who is the same as Lord Krishna, as his devout enemy. Hiranyakashipu wanted to rule the world after all, so he viewed anyone more powerful than himself as an impediment to reaching that goal. Now, to hear his son extolling the virtues of his enemy was too much for the demon to bear. Immediately Hiranyakashipu chastised Prahlada's teachers and asked them who had taught his son these things.

The teachers were taken aback, for they hadn't taught Prahlada anything about Lord Vishnu. This one fact illustrates the difference between a brahmana and a Vaishnava. A brahmana is a priest who is supposed to know Brahman, or the all-pervading impersonal effulgence which contains all things matter and spirit. But just because someone knows Brahman, it doesn't mean that they know Krishna. Though technically there is no difference between Brahman and God, one who remains stuck on the Brahman platform has an inferior angle of vision compared to someone who knows and loves Krishna. That is because Krishna is God's original form as the Supreme Personality of Godhead, the cause of all causes, including Brahman.

Though repeatedly urged by his father to give up this devotion, Prahlada wouldn't budge. Thus Hiranyakashipu decided to have his son killed. He ordered his ministers to kill Prahlada, but the boy seemed to be indestructible. The demon's attendants tried all sorts of different ways to get rid of the young child. The boy was thrown in a pit of fire, hurled off the top of a mountain, thrown in the water, etc. So many different torture methods were tried by the demons, but Prahlada was saved every time just by thinking of Krishna. Finally relenting, Hiranyakashipu allowed Prahlada to go back to school. "If he stays in school, maybe these teachers can finally get through to him." During recess, Prahlada would instruct his fellow classmates on the glories of Lord Vishnu. As a five year old boy, Prahlada was acting as an exemplary spiritual master, giving his classmates the education they were missing out on. Since Prahlada was a Vaishnava, or devotee of Vishnu, he automatically acquired all the knowledge and qualities possessed by a brahmana.

Finally Hiranyakashipu had enough. According to the demon's estimation, no one was able to kill his son, nor was he getting the proper education. Hiranyakashipu decided it was time to personally kill his son. Before going through with the act, Hiranyakashipu threatened Prahlada. Seeing that his son wasn't afraid in the least bit, Hiranyakashipu wanted to know what the source of Prahlada's strength was. After all, Hiranyakashipu's powers came as a result of performing great austerities and receiving benedictions from the demigods. He knew that Prahlada had not gone through such trials and tribulations and thus his power remained a mystery to the demon. Prahlada responded by telling his father that the source of every person's strength is the same: God. The Supreme Lord gives each of us the power to act; He is the original purusha responsible for each person's controlling power.

Hiranyakashipu was getting sick of hearing about Vishnu. He jokingly asked his son that if this Vishnu person was everywhere, was he in the column that was next to them? Hiranyakashipu then punched the column with his hand out of anger. To the surprise of the demon, a huge sound resulted. A terrific form, never before seen, immediately came out of the column. This being resembled a man and a lion, and its arms were spread in all directions. This form, which was Lord Krishna's Narasimhadeva avatara, went on the rampage, killing Hiranyakashipu's associates. Then Narasimhadeva snatched Hiranyakashipu and started punishing the demon. After Hiranyakashipu wailed and moaned, Narasimhadeva let him go. The demigods, who were watching from above, then became afraid since the demon was able to get away. If Narasimhadeva couldn't kill the demon, then who could? Not to worry though, as Krishna was just toying with Hiranyakashipu. Finally, Narasimhadeva took the demon on His lap and bifurcated him with His claws. Hiranyakashipu was dead, and Prahlada was now safe.

The lessons we can take away from this incident are too many to count. That is the greatness of God, for we can discuss His activities from now until the end of time and still never run out of points of interest to ponder over. From the descriptions of this incident found in the Shrimad Bhagavatam, one can't help but notice the gruesome manner in which Hiranyakashipu was killed. There are several animated movies that have been made about Prahlada's life. These movies are obviously intended for all audiences, thus the violence is kept to a minimum. But if we were to accurately portray Hiranyakashipu's killing in cinema, the movie would be too gruesome for even an R rating. This shows just how merciless the Supreme Lord can be if He gets angry.

God is actually quite nice. Though He is neutral towards all living entities, He takes a special interest in the lives of the devotees. In a nutshell, He takes care of His friends. At the same time, those who do harm to His friends will be punished in the worst possible way. Hiranyakashipu tried to kill his son in so many awful ways, so the Lord returned the favor by showing him just how painful death could be. The circumstances of Hiranyakashipu's death were no accident either. Many years prior, the demon had pleased Lord Brahma by performing great austerities. Of course the primary concern for any demon is immortality, so that was the first thing Hiranyakashipu asked from Lord Brahma. Brahma could not grant this wish. Not even Brahma is immortal so how could he grant such a benediction to someone else? Not being satisfied with this, Hiranyakashipu asked for other benedictions that would make him immune from so many different forms of attack. He couldn't be killed at night or in the day, neither in the sky nor on land, nor by any weapon, etc. Being granted so many boons by Brahma, Hiranyakashipu thought he had tricked the great-father into granting him immortality anyway. Hiranyakashipu thought he had all his bases covered, and that there was no way anyone could kill him.

God, however, is smarter than everyone else. The Supreme Lord never likes to make Brahma look like a liar, so He made sure to keep all of Hiranyakashipu's boons intact. Thus the Lord appeared as a half man/half-lion, killing Hiranyakashipu on his lap, using his nails. Thus no human being or entity (living or nonliving) caused his death, nor did the demon die on sea or on land, nor by any weapon. After this incident, Prahlada Maharaja offered some wonderful prayers to pacify the Supreme Lord. The great devotee was then handed the reins of the kingdom.

This incident has been celebrated ever since that time by the devotees of Lord Vishnu. Krishna's most recent incarnation to appear on earth, Lord Chaitanya, was especially fond of the Narasimha avatara. When He would visit the temple of Lord Jagannatha, Lord Chaitanya would pass the deity of Lord Narasimhadeva while climbing up the steps toward the temple. Lord Chaitanya would offer obeissances to Lord Narasimhadeva by reciting specific prayers found in the Narasimha Purana. These prayers are now sung daily in Vaishnava temples around the world.

Narasimhadeva holds a special place in the hearts of devotees due to His causeless mercy and His ability to provide unflinching protection against the attacks of enemies. There is another famous set of prayers, known as the Narasimha-kavacha-stotram, found in the Brahmanda Purana, which was spoken by Prahlada Maharaja. Those who pray to Lord Narasimhadeva regularly, reciting these prayers with great faith and devotion, will be protected from all the demoniac elements of this world. May Lord Narasimhadeva always protect us and may we always follow in the footsteps of the great Bhakta Prahlada.

NARASIMHA CHATURDASHI II

begi boli kulagura, cuau māthe hātha amīke |
sunata ā'i ṛṣi kuśa hare narasiṁha mantra paḍhe, jo
sumirata bhaya bhīke | |

"'Call our family guru immediately to come and touch the child's head with his hands.' Hearing this, the rishi came, and taking some kusha grass to drive away evil spirits, he recited the Narasimha mantra, on hearing which even fear becomes afraid." (Gitavali, 1.12.3)

Mother Kausalya was worried. Her first son, her beloved Raghunandanda, the jewel of the Raghu race, was on this particular day unsteady in His behavior. He was crying and couldn't be pacified by any means. Kausalya tried to feed Him milk, but that wasn't working. A good mother is expert in caring for her beloved child, knowing the proper course of action in many different situations. Since this was no ordinary young boy, the fears of Mother Kausalya increased even more. She tried every remedy she knew, such as worshiping the demigods, the forefathers and the rulers of the different planets, and even giving in charity ghee that was equal in weight to the child; but nothing seemed to work. Finally, she called for the family priest to come and touch her son's head. Hearing of the situation, the rishi quickly arrived on the scene and recited the Narasimha mantra to the child as a way to give Him protection. On the occasion of Narasimha Chaturdashi, we remember and honor the Person addressed in that mantra. His guarantee of protection always applies to the devotees and especially to those who find themselves in helpless conditions, where they seemingly have no recourse but to suffer the wrath inflicted upon them by the wicked.

This particular incident involving Mother Kausalya and her beloved son Rama occurred many thousands of years ago, and the events pertaining to Lord Narasimhadeva, the divine figure whom the mantra chanted by the priest was named after, took place even many millions of years before that. A long time ago, a famous ruler named Hiranyakashipu was wreaking havoc throughout the world.

For a king to be considered powerful and well-respected, his authority and capability to rule must extend across a large region. Even the ordinary individual is the king, or ishvara, of his body, but this kind of control is not very much celebrated or noted. However, if a materially driven individual can put a large subsection of the earth under his control, he will feel like he has real power, that he is really something special.

Hiranyakashipu, through worshiping the self-create, the progenitor of all life on earth, Lord Brahma, received amazing boons that gave him terrific powers. The king at first had asked for immortality, but since even Lord Brahma must take birth and thus eventually die, he is incapable of granting eternal life within the same form of body to anyone. The soul, the essence of life and the basis of individuality, actually lives forever. Never was there a time that the soul did not exist nor will there be a time in the future that it ceases to be. What does go through changes, though, is the outer covering the soul adopts. When someone wants immortality, it is the non-perishability of this covering that they seek. But since the soul is covered by matter, which is an inferior energy, an embodied living being cannot remain in the same state without changing at some point in time.

To get around the inability to receive blanket immortality, Hiranyakashipu figured he would just ask for every other type of boon to cover himself. This behavior is similar to trying to get every grade of protection on your automobile to prevent it from being damaged in a collision or accident. Permanently avoiding accidents on the road is impossible, as the behavior of other drivers is wholly unpredictable. What a car owner can do is try to lower the chances of collision and also the severity of them. Therefore a driver will take many precautions like buying a car that is highly crash resistant, that has enhanced braking systems, and that can safely protect the passengers inside even after impact with another vehicle.

The name Hiranyakashipu means a soft bed or cushion made of gold. The demoniac king wanted to protect his comfortable lifestyle at all costs, and he figured the best way to do that would be to become unbeatable in battle. Therefore he asked Lord Brahma that no living being, large or small, be able to kill him. In addition, he asked that he could not be killed on land or in the sky, in the daytime or at night, nor by any weapon. The demon figured he had every angle covered, but of course no one can outwit the Supreme Lord. When Hiranyakashipu's evil influence would become too strong, as would indeed happen, Vishnu Himself, the Personality of Godhead who has four hands and remains eternally situated in the spiritual sky of Vaikuntha, would come down to earth and show the king just how worthless his boons were.

But first things first; Hiranyakashipu had to enjoy his new powers. He used them to terrorize the world. He was so feared that the demigods, the celestials in charge of different departments of the material creation, descended to earth and took on disguises to keep from being recognized by the king. Hiranyakashipu thought he had everything, for the world was under his control and even the celestials, his greatest enemies, were afraid of him. But as any good ruler will do, he thought about his successor and how his strong arm of control could continue through future generations. Hiranyakashipu wanted his example to be passed down to his children, especially to his first born son, Prahlada.

Though born in the demon race which descended from the womb of Diti, Prahlada took on devotional characteristics from his very birth. While in the womb of his mother, Prahlada heard the instructions offered by Narada Muni, the wonderful saint and devotee of Lord Vishnu. Narada's teachings actually sealed Hiranyakashipu's perilous fate, and they also saved the demigods in the process. For distributing His mercy, the Supreme Lord makes no distinctions on caste, gender or outward features. If He sees that someone is devoted to Him, He becomes their protector forever. With Prahlada's birth came an internal attack to Hiranyakashipu's reign of terror, as the demoniac forces are never any match for the power of divine love.

Born with the divine consciousness, Prahlada worshiped Lord Vishnu without deviation. Even when sent to school to learn about material affairs and how to rule over a kingdom, he still kept

Vishnu and devotion to Him at the forefront of his consciousness. When Hiranyakashipu learned that his son was worshiping his greatest enemy, the object of worship for the demigods, Shri Vishnu, he became incensed. First he tried to get his teachers to change course, but they pled innocent, as they had not taught Prahlada any of the information he was reciting about Vishnu and devotional service, or bhakti-yoga.

Faced with a dilemma, Hiranyakashipu thought it too risky to turn the reigns of the kingdom over to a Vishnu sympathizer. Rather than send his small child elsewhere to continue his devotional efforts, Hiranyakashipu decided that the boy had to be done away with. Simple enough, no? After all, Hiranyakashipu was a powerful king who was feared across the world, so killing a five year old helpless boy should have been a piece of cake. But the demon could not understand that the level of devotion in his son was unmatched, and that simply remembering the Supreme Lord by chanting His names is enough to gain protection from all dangers.

Hiranyakashipu first had the palace guards attack Prahlada with deadly weapons. But since weapons are empowered by Vishnu, they can never do harm to one who is always protected by Him. Then other methods were attempted, such as throwing Prahlada off of a cliff, putting him in a pit of snakes, dropping him to the surface of the ocean and piling rocks on top of him, and placing him in a raging fire. But none of these attempts were successful. Astonished, Hiranyakashipu finally asked his child wherefrom he was getting his powers. After all, Hiranyakashipu had to perform great austerities and please Lord Brahma to get his strength, so the young boy must have done something similar.

Prahlada replied that the source of his strength was the same as that for everyone else, including Hiranyakashipu. Lord Vishnu, as the all-pervading Supersoul, is situated within everyone's heart, and from Him come remembrance, forgetfulness and strength. Aside from angering him, this statement also amused Hiranyakashipu. How could Vishnu be everywhere, especially in a form that wasn't visible? Hiranyakashipu could only see gross matter, thus he had no knowledge of the power of spirit, especially that belonging to the origin of all matter and spirit, God. He then jokingly asked Prahlada if Vishnu was in the column standing next to him. Prahlada had stated that the Lord was indeed in everything, and Hiranyakashipu did not like to hear this. He was prepared to kill his son, but before that he wanted to prove that Vishnu was powerless and certainly not in the column. The king then got up and started banging at the adjacent pillar with his fist.

Little did the demon know that Prahlada was right. As soon as he started punching the column, a terrific figure emerged. It was large and looked like the combination of a man and a lion. This wasn't Vishnu in His original form, but it was the Supreme Lord nonetheless. The scene was so terrible and awe-inspiring that no one could understand what was going on. Thinking that maybe Vishnu had come to kill him in this form of a strange creature, Hiranyakashipu started to attack. But the demon's powers were insignificant compared to the strength of the form of Vishnu known as Narasimhadeva. The Supreme Personality of Godhead, after fighting for a while, finally took the king on His lap and bifurcated him. After Hiranyakashipu was killed, many of the palace soldiers tried to attack Narasimhadeva, but they too were easily killed.

In this way, through his simple and pure devotion to God, Prahlada was saved from all dangers and eventually put on the throne personally by the Supreme Lord. Hiranyakashipu, fear personified, was no match for the most fearful form of Vishnu, Narasimhadeva. Prahlada Maharaja then offered wonderful prayers to his beloved Vishnu, who now stood before him in a wonderful form. Hiranyakashipu's boons all worked as advertised, as Vishnu had not violated any of Brahma's promises. The demon was killed at dusk, so he didn't die during the day or at night. Since he was killed on Narasimhadeva's lap, the demon did not die on land or on water. Narasimhadeva's nails were what killed him, so Hiranyakashipu did not succumb to any weapons.

Prahlada was very touched by Vishnu's personal protection, so he continued his devotion for the rest of his life. In fact, the young child authored a wonderful set of prayers known as the Narasimha-kavacha-stotram, which protects anyone who recites it from danger. There are also other nice prayers calling out to Narasimhadeva found in the Narasimha Purana. Devotees around the world chant and sing these mantras on a daily basis even today. From the time of Hiranyakashipu's slaying, parents following Vedic traditions have protected their young children from evil spirits and the influences of the demoniac by reciting the Narasimha mantra, which immediately calls out to the wonderful figure that protected Prahlada from the wicked forces of his father.

On that wonderful day many millions of years later, the guru of the Raghu dynasty, Vashishta, was called in by Mother Kausalya to protect her child. It was a peculiar day, as the young Rama was crying and not accepting milk. Obviously something must have been wrong; so who better to protect her son than Lord Narasimhadeva. When the guru came to see young Rama, he first took a piece of kusha grass to ward off evil spirits, and then he read the Narasimha mantra. As soon as the child heard this wonderful formula, He giggled slightly, which caused the guru's hair to stand on end. You see this was no ordinary child. Rama was the very same Narasimhadeva, Lord Vishnu, appearing on earth in the form of a prince destined to slay the wicked king ruling Lanka at the time, Ravana.

Former United States President Franklin Delano Roosevelt famously coined the phrase, "The only thing we have to fear is fear itself", during his first inaugural address in 1932. The country was suffering tremendously from the pangs of the Great Depression, so everyone was uncertain about the future. By stating that the only thing worth fearing was the emotion of fear itself, the president hoped to bring some calm and confidence to the citizens of the country. This phrase has since been invoked quite regularly as a rallying cry for those who find themselves in difficult situations and need upliftment.

But some four hundred years prior, Goswami Tulsidas authored an even better phrase, one that references the Supreme Person and His ability to remove anyone's fears. In fact, one of Vishnu's many names is Hari, which means one who removes distresses. When describing the events of that particular day in the kingdom of Ayodhya, Tulsidas says that the guru Vashishta came to protect Rama by reciting the Narasimha mantra, which is so powerful that it even makes fear afraid. Saying that the Narasimha mantra instills fear into fear is a wonderful way to describe the awesome power of the Supreme Lord. Hiranyakashipu was the most feared person on the planet during his time, but he was still no match for Narasimhadeva. Witnessing the gruesome killing of the evil Daitya king who had terrorized the innocent, including his son Prahlada, fear personified learned a great lesson. Fear runs away whenever the name of Narasimhadeva is recited even once.

Lord Rama, as a young child, couldn't help but giggle after He heard the guru recite this glorious mantra. Narasimhadeva's name is so wonderful that even Shri Rama loves to hear it. God takes great joy and delight in seeing His devotees try to protect Him and offer Him service. The name is non-different from the Lord, so anyone who has the good fortune of reciting the name of the Person who saved Prahlada Maharaja will be able to receive the same protections. On Narasimha Chaturdashi, we remember the savior addressed in that wonderful mantra so kindly recited to the young Shri Rama. May we never forget Narasimhadeva, and may He always protect us as we continue our service to Him.

NARASIMHA CHATURDASHI III

As peacefulness and anger are concepts only borne of duality, they are at an equivalent level when associated with true transcendence. The living being is at peace when they think they are in a comfortable situation of life and they are in anger when their pride is hurt or when there is frustration in meeting a desired end. As these are only temporary conditions, to be washed away as quickly as the sand by the next oncoming wave from the ocean, they are not to be overly emphasized within the grander scheme. With the Supreme Lord, whether He is in wonderful peace or extreme anger, the benefit to the affected parties is there all the same. A long time back He was seen by many exalted persons in a terrifying form which had an accompanying angry mood. He looked so fierce that so many powerful personalities, innocent in their own right, dared not approach Him. Yet a young child, who was directly responsible for that form appearing, was brave enough to come forward, not fearing who He knew to be the Supreme Personality of Godhead. That incident which took place eons ago is still celebrated to this day on the occasion of Narasimha Chaturdashi.

Why would God ever get angry? Doesn't that represent a defect to His nature? Anger is not something we strive after. It arises when we lose control of our emotions, so it's usually not a welcomed feeling. Anger is due to frustration, so if the Supreme Lord exhibits this trait does this mean that He is somehow not able to get His way? Actually, the intense emotions shown by the lord of all creatures is for His own pleasure, and once He is pleased naturally those connected to Him in a bond of affection feel supreme delight as well. This fact reinforces the ultimate truth of achintya-bhedabheda-tattva, which says that the living entities are simultaneously one with and different from God.

God is spirit and so are the living entities. The quality of that spirit is the same, as the subordinate group is an expansion of the superior entity. At the same time, the quantitative aspects are vastly different; hence the distinction between the dominant and the dominated. Since the qualitative aspects are equivalent, there is an inherent link between the two groups. Lord Chaitanya Mahaprabhu, who kindly revealed achintya-bhedabheda-tattva, says that the link can be revived through loving devotion, which is best awakened and maintained through the regular chanting of the holy names, "Hare Krishna Hare Krishna, Krishna Krishna, Hare Hare, Hare Rama Hare Rama, Rama Rama, Hare Hare".

When that link is reestablished, every notable action of the Supreme Lord, whether it is occurring in the present or took place many thousands of years ago, gives so much pleasure to the devotee that they feel like they can't get enough. Think of a reservoir of water that constantly gets filled with incoming tributaries but at the same time never overflows. This is how Maharishi Valmiki describes the mood of the devotee with respect to hearing of the qualities and pastimes of their beloved Supreme Lord.

The mood of anger shown a long time ago related to the actions of a demoniac king. Named Hiranyakashipu, the ruler actually appeared in a family of demons, thereby following in the ancestral line with his behavior. Birth in a Daitya family was not considered auspicious because of the lack of potential for developing the devotional consciousness within that race. In the Vedic philosophy there are gradations assigned to birth. These are only from the perspective of potential for achieving the ultimate aim of devotion to the lotus feet of Shri Hari, for the living sparks are the same in quality regardless of the form they adopt. The trees that produce no fruits are considered sinful, while those that do are considered pious. Similarly, within the human species if you take birth in a family of transcendentalists, it is considered a boon because of the spiritual environment that you can grow up in, which in turn increases the chances of a fruitful life.

Birth in a family of demons is very unfortunate because not only is spiritual culture lacking, but the tendency is to take to sinful life - stealing, cheating, killing and the like. By following these behaviors the spirit soul actually goes backward in the chain of reincarnation, sort of like travelling in the wrong direction in a race. Hiranyakashipu lived up to his family's reputation and then some.

He developed tremendous powers as a result of asking for boons from those who can grant them. Any ability can be exercised in one of two ways: correctly or incorrectly. The ability itself is not to blame, but rather the person who invokes it incorrectly.

Hiranyakashipu took his boons received from Lord Brahma as an opportunity to take over the world. He defeated so many powerful rulers that no one dared fight him in battle. The world lived in fear of him, and he thought that he was the supreme being. In his mind, there was no God, and if the person who everyone thought was God really were, He would descend to earth and put up a challenge to the king's authority. The king's eventual demise was set in motion with the birth of his son Prahlada. Though born in a Daitya family, the young child heard about devotional service while within the womb of his mother. The great servant of Narayana, Narada Muni, instructed the pregnant woman on devotion, and the unborn Prahlada heard and remembered those instructions. Thus he was born a devotee.

Hiranyakashipu hated this trait in his son so much that after a while the boy's stubbornness became too much to bear. Despite his best efforts, Hiranyakashipu couldn't convince Prahlada to give up his devotion to Vishnu, which is the name for God that addresses His all-pervasiveness. Vishnu was the king's enemy, so seeing this devotion in his son was like getting a dagger through the heart. Unable to accept it any longer, Hiranyakashipu ordered his assistants to kill the five-year old boy.

One slight problem though. Prahlada was unbreakable. He was thrown off a cliff, put into a pit of snakes, taken into a raging fire, and dropped to the bottom of an ocean. The successive attempts were only necessary because the previous ones didn't work. Prahlada couldn't be harmed because during every attack he thought of his Vishnu in a mood of love. The child had no other protection. He didn't have fighting ability or strength. No one intervened from the outside due to fear of Hiranyakashipu. Thus it was only Vishnu who saved the boy each time.

The anger from the Supreme Lord came when He had enough of Hiranyakashipu's attempts. Vishnu took on the form of a half-man/half-lion to respect the boons of safety previously offered to Hiranyakashipu by Lord Brahma. This ferocious and unique form appeared on the scene and quickly killed all of Hiranyakashipu's guards. Then the demon-king himself would be snatched by Narasimhadeva and placed on His lap, just as Garuda, the king of birds, grabs a snake to eat. Hiranyakashipu would be bifurcated by Narasimhadeva's nails, thus dying in a most gruesome way.

After the demon king was killed, Narasimhadeva was still seething with rage. Many demigods tried to pacify Him with prayers, but nothing seemed to work. Finally, Lord Brahma asked Prahlada to approach Narasimhadeva. Prahlada was a young boy after all, and Vishnu was there specifically to save him. Thus He couldn't keep that angry mood when talking to the young, innocent child.

Prahlada did as he was asked, and he wasn't afraid at all. Rather, he was so delighted to see the Supreme Lord come to his rescue. He knew that the angry mood was for Vishnu's own pleasure, which in turn pleased those who are devoted to Him. Prahlada then offered a wonderful set of prayers, which pleased Narasimhadeva so much that He offered Prahlada many material benedictions in return. Prahlada only wanted devotion, being afraid of material entanglement. Hearing this pleased Narasimhadeva even more, so He guaranteed Prahlada that he would get conditions auspicious for devotional service despite remaining in material association.

That wonderful event from ancient times is celebrated annually on the occasion of Narasimha Chaturdashi. Though there was tremendous violence involved, since it related to Bhagavan and His protection of the saintly Prahlada, it is as pleasurable to hear about as a more peaceful event. Prahlada knew there was nothing to fear with that ferocious form, as its anger was directed only at the miscreant Hiranyakashipu and his supporters. In this life the real cause of fear is the continuation of a life not devoted to God, one where temporary pleasures are mistakenly taken to be permanent. Know from Prahlada that devotional service is the life's mission and that it can be adopted by any person, from any place. Whether in an outwardly angry or peaceful mood, the Supreme Lord will accept sincere devotional offerings and be pleased to the heart by them.

In Closing:

In a rage after killing Prahlada's father,
Thus no one dared Narasimhadeva to bother.

"Dear Prahlada, so that the Lord's anger can be eased,
Please approach Him, with your prayers He'll be pleased."

Brahma these instructions to young boy gave,
Because knew Narasimha came for Prahlada to save.

From prayers supreme favor of God did earn,
Received material benedictions in return.

But to Prahlada material life a great fear,
Away from lotus feet of God it would steer.

Narasimha explained and dispelled any doubts,
Prahlada, never divine love to live without.

KRISHNA JANMASHTAMI I

Janmashtami is the appearance day celebration of Lord Krishna, the Supreme Personality of Godhead. The appearance day is the equivalent of the birthday, except that since God never actually takes birth, the occasions of His advents on earth are referred to as appearances. Celebrating the anniversary of this day is important because not everyone has the time nor the dedication to always think about God. In reality, every day should be treated as Krishna's birthday, for His blessings are around us at all times. Yet by just remembering the Lord's appearance and His transcendental activities, one makes great progress towards the ultimate spiritual perfection, that of thinking of the Lord at the time of death. Just a little service, a small exchange of sincere emotion and love, directed at the Lord can prove to be pivotal in turning our fortunes around. This principle was illustrated in one small incident during the Lord's youth.

When we speak of Krishna's youth, it is in reference to the timeline of His stay on earth. Around five thousand years ago, there was a powerful king named Kamsa who was ruling over Mathura, a town in what is presently known as India. During those times, "back in the day" so to speak, there was no such thing as India. The land was called Bharatavarsha, for the inhabitants of that land were descendants of the great King Bharata. Sometimes when a king or military leader is very successful or popular, the land will be named after him. This is true nowadays of celebrity figures as well. A famous baseball player, musician, or politician will have streets, buildings, and bridges named after them. Maharaja Bharata was so great that the entire planet was named after him.

Though he was the King of Mathura, Kamsa's presence was felt in the neighboring lands as well. He crafted strategic alliances with other kings as a way to consolidate his power. Normally this kind of reign isn't a bad thing. If we have a pious king, one who is dedicated to the welfare of the innocent, it would surely be a good thing to have that king's presence felt in as large an area as possible. Sadly, this was not the case with Kamsa. From the Shrimad

Bhagavatam, the crown jewel of Vedic literature, we understand that Kamsa was formerly a pious soul who made a transgression that caused him to be thrown into the material world. Upon landing in this temporary and miserable place where God is forgotten and man is allured by the energy known as maya, Kamsa assumed all demonic qualities. He was pious from time to time, but his underlying nature was that of a demon. This was by design, for Lord Krishna Himself was destined to come to earth to kill him. When Krishna fights with enemies, His adversaries are no ordinary human beings. Since they act as God's sparring partners, these demons are some of the most exalted personalities.

Kamsa was made aware of his future fate at the most unexpected of moments. His sister Devaki had just gotten married to a kshatriya named Vasudeva. In Vedic style marriages, or in any traditional type of marriage, the bride is deemed to be given away to the groom's family. Since that is the case, the marriage ceremony represents the parting of the girl from the family she grew up with. To ease the pain of separation, the tradition is that the bride's brother will usually escort her, along with her husband, to her new home. This is what occurred with Kamsa and Devaki. During their ride to Vasudeva's home, a voice in the sky proclaimed that Devaki's eighth son would kill Kamsa. Shocked to hear this announcement, Kamsa took out his sword and was ready to kill his sister immediately. This was certainly strange behavior, for Devaki had done nothing wrong. Yet not wanting to risk future injury, Kamsa lost all sense of rationale. Vasudeva kindly stepped in and was able to pacify Kamsa with clever words. Vasudeva offered to give up each one of Devaki's sons to Kamsa as a sign of good faith. This way, the husband and wife could go on living, and Kamsa's fears could be alleviated.

Day and night Kamsa thought about Devaki's eighth son. He couldn't sleep, he couldn't eat, whatever he would do, wherever he would go, he would simply think about this eighth child. Not wanting to take any chances, Kamsa had Vasudeva and Devaki locked up in a jail. With every child that was born to Devaki, Kamsa would take it and throw it against a stone wall. There is much controversy today about the abortion issue, where the child is killed within the womb through some medical procedure. Kamsa didn't mess around with that idea; he went straight for infanticide. Leaving no room for doubt, he killed the infants in the worst possible way. One certainly has to be the greatest barbarian to take to such action.

When Devaki finally gave birth to her eighth child, it was in the middle of the night, at midnight to be more exact. This was no ordinary child; it was the Supreme Personality of Godhead Himself. Krishna came to earth to save Devaki and Vasudeva, who technically became His biological parents. In order to reveal His divine nature to His parents, Krishna appeared in His four-handed form of Lord Vishnu. Devotees of Vishnu are known as Vaishnavas. Since there is no difference between Krishna and Vishnu, for they are the same original God, devotees of Krishna are also known as Vaishnavas. After offering wonderful prayers to Vishnu, both Devaki and Vasudeva began to worry about what Kamsa would do. Krishna was their savior after all, so if Kamsa were to kill Him, all hope would be lost. Krishna's parents asked Him to hide His true form out of fear of Kamsa. The Lord then requested Vasudeva to transfer Him to the nearby town of Gokula, which was headed by Nanda Maharaja.

In the dead of night, while all the guards were sleeping, the Supreme Personality of Godhead, in His blissful, love-evoking infant form, was taken by Vasudeva from Mathura to Gokula. Though the guards were asleep and the shackles removed from Vasudeva, the path to Gokula was not without impediment. There was a strong storm which threatened to obstruct Vasudeva's path across a raging river. Yet miraculously, Ananta Shesha Naga, the serpent bed of Lord Vishnu in the spiritual sky, appeared on the scene and acted as an umbrella for Krishna and Vasudeva. Just as Shri Lakshmana had stood alongside Lord Rama many thousands of years before, the same Ananta Shesha Naga came to protect Rama in His form of Krishna. As he waded through the Yamuna River, which had kindly allowed for Krishna's passage, Vasudeva held his son above his head so as to keep Krishna safe from the water. With Ananta Shesha Naga acting as the umbrella for both of them, the scene became quite a memorable one. On the day of

Janmashtami, this scene of the three great personalities travelling to Gokula is often remembered by Vaishnavas.

Upon reaching Gokula, Vasudeva dropped Krishna off at Nanda Maharaja's house, while at the same time taking the baby girl who had just been born to Nanda's wife Yashoda. A short while after Vasudeva's return to Mathura with the little girl, Kamsa found out about the birth of Devaki's eighth child. Even though the prophecy said that it would be Devaki's eighth son to kill him, Kamsa wasn't going to take any chances. When he was about ready to throw the girl on the stone slab, the child slipped out of his hands and took to the sky. The child revealed her true form, that of Goddess Durga, the faithful servant of Lord Krishna and controller of the material energy. She laughed at Kamsa and told him that his angel of death had already appeared in this world and was ready to kill him. Though over the next few years Kamsa would try his best to have the child Krishna killed, he would be unsuccessful in his attempts. Eventually Krishna would come to Mathura and kill Kamsa and thus fulfill the prophecy.

Krishna's childhood in Gokula and Vrindavana is what the devotees are especially fond of. The residents of these towns loved Krishna. This was especially true of Krishna's foster-parents Nanda and Yashoda. There are so many incidents from Krishna's childhood that evoke emotions of love and attachment; so one can learn great lessons from all of them. One incident in particular really crystallizes the relationship between the devotee and God and what it takes to keep this relationship intact.

Nanda Maharaja belonged to the farming community, technically known as the vaishyas. The Vedic system for societal maintenance calls for four divisions, or classes, of men. The third division is the vaishya, and their duty is to engage in agriculture, banking, cow protection, and general commerce. The four divisions can be thought of in terms of the different work prescribed to employees of a successful company. In any profitable company, there will be different people engaged in different work. Some people will serve as the leaders; they will be in charge of the big picture, determining what the future course of action will be. There are others who serve as the laborers; they will take to the nitty-gritty, hard labor. Others will be involved in assessing risk and running analysis on profits and future outlooks. Others will be the brains of the productivity side; they will write software and manage the human and physical assets. For the company to be successful, each person must do the job they are best suited for. If a person is suited to be a leader, it would be silly to put them in charge of the hard labor, the nuts and bolts of the operation. If a person is suited to be a salesmen, it would be silly to put them in charge of writing software and doing work that didn't involve human interaction.

By the same token, a successful and peaceful society requires the cooperation of all four divisions. Since Nanda Maharaja belonged to the mercantile division, he and his family spent most of their time engaged in cow protection. If one keeps a few cows protected and well-maintained, they can have all of their economic problems solved. Nanda Maharaja's family also took part in agriculture, so they had a decent stock of grain in their house. Grain, milk, butter, yogurt, etc., are all that is needed to survive in this world. There is no need for the eating of animal flesh when these commodities are in good supply.

On one occasion, a fruit vendor came to Nanda's house. At the time, Krishna was very young; He could barely walk or speak. Krishna delighted everyone around Him, especially when He took to imitating the activities of the adults. It is quite common to see young children try to imitate the activities of adults, and Krishna was no different in this regard. The fruit vendor had a surplus supply of various fruits, so they would go out and sell the surplus around town. The buying and selling during those times took place through the barter system. This also teaches us how currencies work. The currency of a given area can actually be anything. In times past, the currencies of particular areas have been gold coins, seashells, and even cigarettes.

When this fruit vendor would come to Nanda's house, they would receive grains in exchange for the fruit. Obviously there would be a certain amount of grain needed to purchase a certain amount of fruit. Whatever was peaceably and voluntarily agreed upon was the going exchange rate. Lord Krishna must have seen these exchanges going on from time to time. On one particular occasion, baby Krishna decided to make His own exchange. He grabbed a small handful of grains and eagerly approached the vendor to make the trade. Since He was a small child, obviously He couldn't fit much grain into His hands. To make matters worse, while running towards the vendor, much of the grain fell out of Krishna's hands. The small child was a little despondent upon seeing that He didn't have much to offer the fruit vendor, but the vendor was so taken by Krishna's sincerity that they made the exchange anyway. The Supreme Personality of Godhead kindly offered some grains with love and sincerity, and this was all the fruit vendor needed. This was deemed a fair exchange.

After giving Krishna the fruit, the vendor looked at their basket and saw that all the fruit had been transformed into valuable jewels. Everyone was quite astonished and they couldn't figure out what had happened. The vendor, who was honest, sincere, and a pure devotee of Krishna, offered some small fruits to Krishna and was rewarded with jewels. Obviously as an honest and humble person, the fruit vendor didn't require these jewels, but the Lord wanted to make them happy. With a more valuable commodity, the vendor wouldn't have to worry so much about making a living.

This one incident is a great reminder of the meaning of life and how we can go about utilizing everything in our possession the proper way. Since God is the creator, He is the original owner of everything. All of our possessions, bodily attributes, and familial relationships are due to Krishna's mercy. The Lord offered the fruit vendor a small quantity of grain, but the Lord has already given us much more. The fruit vendor was more than satisfied with this blessing from the Lord, so they returned the favor by parting with something that was valuable to them, a commodity which was the source of their livelihood. By the same token, we should be equally as kind to the Lord by offering Him everything in our possession, including those things we value the most. The most valuable thing that we own is time, so this is what we should sacrifice to the Lord.

The best way to give our time to Krishna is to chant the Lord's holy names, "Hare Krishna Hare Krishna, Krishna Krishna, Hare Hare, Hare Rama Hare Rama, Rama Rama, Hare Hare". This chanting process is most sublime because it takes care of hearing, speaking, and remembering. Moreover, it is a sacrifice, the yajna of of all yajnas. On Janmashtami Day, and on every other day of the year, we should make the necessary sacrifice to spend time with Krishna. Just as the fruit vendor had their ordinary commodity turned into valuable jewels, the chanting sacrifice will reward us with the beautification of everything in our lives, including our own bodies. At the time of death, our soul will get an upgrade of bodies, from a temporary and miserable one to an eternally blissful and spiritual one. This spiritual body will allow us to associate with Krishna all the time, thus enabling us to derive the same pleasure felt by the residents of Gokula.

KRISHNA JANMASHTAMI II

Immerse yourself in the transcendental nectar made up of the eternal pastimes of Lord Shri Krishna, the Supreme Personality of Godhead, the most attractive person in any room He walks into. Every person is predisposed towards worshiping, but unless that inkling is matched with the worthiest recipient, the search for real pleasure will futilely continue. Yet just by hearing about the Supreme Lord, especially in His original form of Krishna, the awakening of the dormant God consciousness resting within the heart can become a reality in a second. Krishna should be remembered every single day, for do we forgo eating, sleeping or having fun on most days? If routine work follows a schedule, then why shouldn't our worship of Krishna, the greatest source of pleasure? Even if there are impediments inhibiting daily worship, such as the tendency to view religious life as a chore instead of a delight, just remember Krishna on Janmashtami, once a year on the anniversary that marks His appearance in this wonderful world.

How can we declare this world to be wonderful? Just turning on the news reveals evidence of how not wonderful this place is. Natural disasters, lying politicians, gruesome murderers living around the block, and so many other horrible sites leave us asking the question, "Why am I here? Why is life so bad?" Yet the paramahamsas, the topmost transcendentalists, consider this place, or any place for that matter, wonderful because it comes from the Lord. Moreover, though He is not personally involved in the daily operations of a land separated from Him, God will still periodically make appearances. Just as the sun rises and sets at regular intervals, the time period of creation when viewed from the perspective of a day has regularly scheduled appearances by the Supreme Lord. Janmashtami celebrates Shri Krishna's descent to this phenomenal land in His personal self, without any need of changing His form or highlighting certain qualities.

What do we mean by this? Every life form, an autonomous spark directed by the spirit soul within, comes from God. If Krishna is so pure and perfect, how can those things which expand from Him be deficient? Doesn't this reveal a flaw in the Creator? The expansions are also eternally existing entities, but their constitutional position is a little different. God is the superior and His expansions are the inferior. There are different gradations of expansions, with some not even having any intelligence. The internal potency expansions are like Krishna in quality, while the external expansions are material, not having any spiritual identity. The living entities are part of Krishna's superior energy, but they can choose in favor of the external energy's association.

To aid the marginal potency fragments in choosing in favor of returning to the Lord's association, Krishna periodically comes to earth in various non-different forms. These are personal expansions, while the living entities are referred to as separated expansions. The avataras, or incarnations, are fully endowed with Krishna's features and they can attract the hearts and minds of the pure hearted saints. The difference between a saint and a wicked character can be seen in the type of pain they inflict. Both the good and the bad cause pain to others, but the saints cause pain by their separation and the miscreants by their presence. Similarly, when Krishna's incarnations appear on earth, they inflict pain on the nefarious characters trying to stamp out any presence of religion in the world. While He roams the land, the Lord gives pleasure to His devotees, but when He leaves there is tremendous pain. Separation anxiety from Krishna is so acute that the pain actually ends up being beneficial, sort of like the "hurts so good" concept.

To alleviate the pain of separation caused by Krishna's absence, the devotees try to remember the Lord as often as possible. Thankfully the kind-hearted saints of the past documented the activities of Krishna's avatars in wonderful texts like the Ramayana and Puranas. On Janmashtami, devotees remember the appearance and activities of Krishna Himself, the Supreme Lord coming to earth in His original form. The descriptions of Krishna's life and pastimes on earth are found in many texts, including the Harivamsha and Mahabharata, but they are best sequenced together in the tenth canto of the sacred Shrimad Bhagavatam, which is also known as the Bhagavata Purana.

What was so memorable about Krishna's time on earth? For starters, His birth was not ordinary. For Krishna, there is never birth or death. Actually, the same holds true for the living entities, as nothing can kill the imperishable soul. Birth and death really refer to the spirit soul's acceptance and rejection of bodies through reincarnation, which is fueled by karma. This doesn't apply to Krishna, however, as everything He does is at His own whim. His birth in the prison cell in Mathura was at His choosing, as His parents Mother Devaki and Vasudeva had previously undergone many austerities to become qualified to have God come as their son.

The parents were in prison because Kamsa wanted to kill Devaki's eighth child, for it had been prophesized that this child would lead to the king's death. Since Krishna appeared at midnight, Janmashtami is a full day celebration, with the festivities culminating at night with the clock striking twelve to mark the occasion of the Lord's emergence from Devaki's womb. To show that He was the Supreme Lord, Krishna displayed His Vishnu form, which has four hands and is opulently adorned. Afraid of what Kamsa would do, the parents were eager to protect Krishna. The Lord then advised Vasudeva to transfer Him to the neighboring town of Vrindavana, where Yashoda, the wife of King Nanda, had just given birth to a daughter. Krishna would go to Vrindavana and the daughter would be placed in the prison cell.

The girl was Durga Devi, Lord Shiva's wife who is in charge of this material creation, which is thus known as Devi-dhama. She is known as Durga because her energy, material nature, is very difficult to overcome. She would give a glimpse of this difficulty to Kamsa, who tried to throw her against a stone wall when he found out that Devaki had delivered another child. But before he could kill her, the child slipped out of his hands and went into the sky, taking on a beautiful form with eight hands. She then warned Kamsa that the child he had feared so much had actually been born already.

Meanwhile in Vrindavana, everyone marveled at the young child seemingly delivered by Mother Yashoda. Krishna is described as maha-tejah in the Vedas, which means that He is marvelously resplendent. He has this glow about Him that follows Him wherever He goes. Of all the pastimes enacted by Krishna, it would be hard to argue against His childhood pranks in Vrindavana being the most endearing. Just think of how much pleasure parents derive from their own children walking about, trying to crawl, trying to say their first words, getting in trouble, etc. Now add to the fact that your child is the Supreme Lord Himself, and you can begin to imagine just how happy Nanda and Yashoda felt at having their most wonderful blessing in their lives.

Krishna's elder brother Balarama was also raised in Vrindavana. Both Krishna and Balarama were sons of Vasudeva and Devaki, though they were raised in Vrindavana to avoid Kamsa in the early years. Balarama is the same Ananta Shesha Naga, the serpent bed on whom Lord Vishnu resides in the spiritual sky. Krishna and Balarama did everything together in their childhood, including play different pranks and exhibit naughty behavior. When they began to crawl, they would both regularly get dirt on their bodies. Krishna was raised in Vrindavana by Mother Yashoda and Balarama by Mother Rohini. The mothers would smear their children with saffron in the morning, but by midday the boys would be covered with dirt and come to their mothers. All the hard work of preparation had gone for naught, but seeing their children so happily engaged in play gave the mothers endless delight.

Vrindavana was a farm community, so there were many cows around. The milk products produced by the cows would be used to maintain the citizens. Thus the cows were honored, respected and taken care of. As is natural for young, curious children, Krishna and Balarama would make their way to the different places in the community that were mysterious and unknown to them, places that adults regularly went. The cowshed was obviously one of these places. Krishna and Balarama would make their way to where the cows were and grab their tails. An adult cow is rather large compared to a child that can't even walk yet, so we can just imagine what would happen next.

The cows, feeling the pressure on their tails, would then run away. Krishna and Balarama of course did not let go. Hence they would go for a ride in the mud and cow dung, similar to how people "jet ski" on the water for fun. Seeing the beautiful Krishna and Balarama roaming around in the mud like this brought great delight to the mothers and the gopis, the cowherd women of the community. They would huddle up together to enjoy the fun. Actually, just remembering this sight every day is enough to cure the most punishing mental ailment. To be given the chance to witness this, the gopis had to be extremely pious and fortunate. The Supreme Lord, who cannot be caught by the penances of ascetics, the meditation of yogis, or the study of Vedantists, was being dragged around by cows through the mud of Vrindavana. Transcendental love ruled over the community.

As time went by, Krishna would fulfill the prophesy known to Kamsa about his death. More pastimes would occur later on in life as well, but Krishna's time spent in Vrindavana is what the devotees remember the most. Janmashtami allows any person of any religious persuasion to bask in the delightful sound vibrations of Krishna-katha. Just by regularly hearing about Krishna, one is sure to become a devotee. One who never forgets the beautiful Shyamasundara, the youth who roamed the sacred land of Vrindavana with Balarama and had the complexion of a dark raincloud, will find felicity in both this life and the next.

KRISHNA JANMASHTAMI III

Ignorance is darkness and knowledge is light, and so the spirit soul encased in gross and subtle material elements lives in darkness until the true light of knowledge of its inherent relationship to the Supreme is revealed. The revelation can come at any moment, and when it does, the connection to the divine creates a link in consciousness that doesn't have to break. The realized soul knows that God is with them, so the cloud of nescience never has to return. The transcendental light can come internally through the practice of yoga or externally through the direct presence of Shri Krishna Himself, who showed the power of His effulgence moments after appearing from the womb of mother Devaki. That wonderful incident is still celebrated to this day on the occasion of Shri Krishna Janmashtami.

Krishna is God. Not a deity of sectarian importance or a mythological character of the Hindu faith, Lord Krishna is the Supreme Personality of Godhead. His name speaks to His all-attractiveness. Krishna's smile is so enchanting that it takes away the pride of the staunchest devotee of material nature. The sweetness of the sounds emanating from His flute capture the attention of human beings and animals alike. The peacock feather in His hair and the kaustubha gem around His neck keep the eyes focused on His transcendental form. To meditate on Him is the most worthwhile activity for the eyes, which are gifts from nature to be used in the proper way.

The all-attractive vision is granted to the population of the earth periodically when Krishna decides to appear. He states in the Bhagavad-gita that one of the reasons for His advents is to annihilate the miscreants. The miscreant in this case refers to an enemy of religion, someone who purposefully thwarts the harmless efforts in spirituality of the saintly class. Accompanying the elimination of the miscreant influence is the reinstatement of the religious principles. The highest religious principle is bhakti-yoga, or devotion to God, and so that devotion is reinstituted best when there is the direct vision of the Supreme Lord.

During the Dvapara Yuga, a famous miscreant was ruling over the town of Mathura. A prophecy had stated that his sister's eighth child would kill him. Not wanting to take any chances, King Kamsa imprisoned his sister Devaki and her husband Vasudeva. Each of her first seven children was then killed by Kamsa immediately after they were born. Ah, but the prophecy would hold true nonetheless, as Devaki's eighth child was Krishna Himself. When He emerged from the mother's womb, Krishna first showed His four-handed form of Lord Vishnu, which indicated to the parents that their son was God Himself arriving on the scene to grant them special favor.

Despite seeing Vishnu, the parents were worried that Kamsa would come and kill their newborn child. Knowing this, Krishna asked Vasudeva to transfer Him to the nearby town of Gokula, which was a farm community. Kamsa would not find out about Krishna's birth until later on, and so nothing bad could happen in the meantime. Even if it did, young Krishna, though in the body of an infant, would save the day.

As if to show the magic of His transcendental form, Krishna's effulgence spread immediately. The Lord appeared at midnight in a jail cell, while the outside guards were asleep. Vasudeva was to transfer the child to Gokula immediately; there was no time to waste. The problem was that it was dark outside. How was the father going to see without some kind of external lighting? He didn't want to draw attention to himself either; as no one was to know where he was going.

When Vasudeva took Krishna in his lap, suddenly he could see everywhere. This wasn't a magic trick. The boy wasn't holding a secret lamp. He is naturally effulgent. It is said that the light of Brahman, which represents the sum collection of spiritual fragments in the material universe, emanates from the gigantic body of the Supreme Lord. He is the source of all light, and we know that darkness is only the absence of light. Holding Krishna in His arms, Vasudeva had no problem seeing. Even when he had to cross over the Yamuna river and it started to rain, Krishna's trusted servant,

Ananta Shesha Naga, arrived on the scene to create an umbrella of protection with his many hoods.

Krishna's transcendental effulgence also exists in stories about Him, including the accounts of His initial appearance in Mathura. It also exists in His holy name. Therefore the illuminating spiritual practice for the modern age, which is applicable to any person in any part of the world, is the chanting of the holy names, "Hare Krishna Hare Krishna, Krishna Krishna, Hare Hare, Hare Rama Hare Rama, Rama Rama, Hare Hare".

Krishna Janmashtami is the time to remember Krishna and the influence He had in both Gokula and Mathura. Kamsa would eventually find out about His birth and he would try every which way to kill Krishna. But the Lord can never be annihilated, and conversely nothing could be done to save Kamsa, who was destined to die at the hands of the delight of Devaki. That sweetheart son protected His parents, eventually freeing them from prison and allowing them to live in peace. To always keep the vision of the owner of all matter and spirit in your mind is the way to remain in the light, and to celebrate His appearance on Janmashtami is the way to further reinforce that remembrance for the days that lay ahead.

In Closing:

After child's birth Lord Vishnu they saw,
Appeared from Devaki's womb, kept them in awe.

From King Kamsa Krishna needed to be safe,
So boy to Gokula father Vasudeva would take.

But there was a problem in limited sight,
In dead of night father required light.

Krishna's body automatically is bright,
Effulgent is Vasudeva and Devaki's delight.

Through the darkness, God to show the way,

Remember His name and glories on Janmashtami day.

VYASA PUJA I

How do we find God? How do we find the proper path in life, that road which will lead us to the promise land? Many people have answers, but who should we believe? The Vedas, the ancient scriptures of India, tell us that the answers to life's most troubling questions are only known to a select few exalted individuals. These individuals, though they may come in different shapes, sizes, and overall appearances, carry what is lacking to the bewildered soul. These individuals are known as gurus, or spiritual masters, and one who humbly approaches them can have all of life's problems solved.

Simply put, the spiritual master is a representative of God. Just as a king or government leader has trusted aides and officers, the Supreme Lord has His representatives on earth. On a more basic level, the guru is a teacher, except that the subject matter they teach is more important than that of any other teacher's. For one to teach, they have to know. If someone doesn't know how to do something, their teaching will not be effective. The spiritual master teaches others about God, how to find Him, and then how to serve Him. This last point is the most important: serving God. The basic teaching of the bona fide spiritual masters - those who are friends, servants, and surrendered souls to the Supreme Personality of Godhead, Lord Krishna - is that the individual spirit souls are fragmental sparks emanating from the original and gigantic fire known as God. As individual sparks, the wayward spirit souls are similar in quality to the original fire, but vastly inferior in quantity. True bliss, enlightenment, and peace of mind can only be achieved when the sparks return to the original fire, signaling a return to their original habitat so to speak. Upon entering this original realm, the activities of the sparks do not cease, but rather become purified. This purified activity is known as devotional service, or bhakti-yoga.

Judging who is a bona fide spiritual master and who isn't is quite straightforward. We simply have to tell if a person is surrendered to Krishna or not. We can think of it in this way: Celebrities and star athletes all have agents. These representatives negotiate deals on behalf of their client with higher ups, wealthy franchises, and movie studios. It's easier to have an agent haggle about dollars and cents than it is for the person to go themselves and squabble with their potential bosses. A good agent is one who represents the interests of their client and not themselves. Naturally, if the client is satisfied, the agent will be as well. The same principle applies to spiritual masters. If a guru is working only on behalf of Krishna, then naturally the Lord will be happy, which will also result in the guru's happiness.

How does a guru determine what Krishna wants? The answer to this is quite simple as well. A guru has learned the art from their own guru, who learned it from their guru, and so on. Traversing the chain of spiritual masters all the way to the top, one will eventually reach Krishna, or God. This is the other component to determining the bona fides of the spiritual master. If their unbroken chain of disciplic succession doesn't eventually reach Krishna, their teachings cannot be considered legitimate. At the same time, this chain also cannot be broken through any deviation in teachings. As mentioned before, the guru's main business is to please Krishna. As strangers trapped in a strange land, the spiritual sparks represented by the individual living entities are lost and unaware of the ultimate purpose in life. The transcendent Lord's happiness comes through reclaiming His lost souls and having them return to their original home. The guru, as the via-medium, is tasked with creating the mode of transport, taking the individual souls to the point of entry into the spiritual world. In this way, the guru is the ocean of mercy, a transcendental boatman who can carry the wayward souls back to their original destination.

What's interesting to note is that the most exalted of gurus actually don't need to produce proof of their disciplic succession in order to be successful in their efforts. Since the message they carry is so pure and powerful, they can deliver fallen souls simply through their instructions. An example of one such powerful guru is Narada Muni. The son of Lord Brahma, who is the first-created living entity and thus original spiritual master of the world, Narada Muni is probably the greatest reformer in the history of mankind. Vedic literature is full of incidents relating to Narada's healing powers. Because Narada is a great saint and spiritual master, his disciples serve as the who's who of Vedic writers, poets, and gurus.

A long long time ago, there was a dacoit living in the forest, earning his living by killing people and robbing them of their wealth. This dacoit one day happened to attempt to rob Narada Muni. As a sannyasi [one in the renounced order of life], Narada does not carry anything with him except for his vina, which is a type of musical instrument. Narada has the ability to travel the three worlds, so he makes the most of this power by spreading Lord Narayana's glories throughout the world. Lord Krishna is considered God's original form, but Narayana is essentially on equal footing with Krishna; He's just the four-handed version of God. If one simply devotes themselves to Vishnu or Narayana, they are equally worshiping the original Supreme Lord.

So Narada came upon this dacoit and asked him why he was stealing. Since Narada was a mendicant, he had nothing to offer the thief. After asking the dacoit some insightful questions, to which the dacoit had no tangible answers, Narada convinced him to sit in meditation and chant the name of Rama. While Vishnu is the same as the original form of Godhead, so is Lord Rama, who is considered an avatara of Lord Vishnu. Devotees of Krishna, Vishnu, or any other non-different form of God are known as Vaishnavas. In the Vedic tradition, devotees typically pick one form and devote themselves completely to Him. For example, great authors and saints like Shrila Rupa Gosvami, Sanatana Gosvami, and their disciples worship Lord Krishna along with His pleasure potency Shrimati Radharani. They are not really interested in worshiping God in any other form, except for maybe His preacher incarnation of Lord Chaitanya. Devotees like Goswami Tulsidas, however, only see God as Lord Rama. Tulsidas actually makes many references to incidents relating to Lord Krishna, Vishnu, and other avataras in his writings, but he does so in the mood of devotion to Rama. To Tulsidas, there is no other God except Rama.

In this respect, anyone who takes to worship of Krishna, Rama, Narasimha, or any other vishnu-tattva form is worshiping the original form of Godhead. So Narada advised this dacoit to chant Lord Rama's name, but the dacoit was not able to do so at the time. He wasn't properly conditioned to chant the transcendental name of the Lord; a name which is non-different from the original form of God. Narada, ever the wise guru, told the dacoit not to worry and to chant "mara" instead. This word means death. Now what kind of spiritual master would advise his student to chant the word "death" over and over again? Ah, but there was a method to this apparent madness. By chanting "mara" over and over again, the dacoit actually was saying the name of Rama without knowing it. We can actually try this ourselves. If we say "mara" over and over again and limit the gaps in between the words, we'll actually be saying "Rama". Pretty soon, through regular, coincidental chanting of the name of God, the dacoit gained enlightenment. Since his meditation through chanting was so great, he didn't even notice the anthill that had formed around him. Upon seeing this, Narada named the dacoit Valmiki, meaning one who is born from an anthill. The rest was history as Valmiki went on to author the original biography of Lord Rama known as the Ramayana. This poem and Valmiki himself are celebrated to this day.

This is just one example of Narada's healing powers. He similarly has performed the same magic with other disciples. We should take note of the fact that these disciples don't ask for Narada's resume when he comes to teach them. His message is so powerful that simply through his teaching he can deliver anyone. The key component to success is the willingness of the disciple to listen to the guru's words. This also raises another important point. Contrary to the thought of many, no one can tell anyone else who their guru is. Surely one can make the attempt, sincere or otherwise, to persuade another into surrendering to a specific exalted personality, but that surrender will be meaningless if the disciple is not wholeheartedly in favor of following the guru's instructions. No one forced the dacoit to listen to Narada Muni. The dacoit listened to the great sage's words and then decided to surrender himself completely to him and his instructions. In this way, through voluntary and humble submission, the great Valmiki was made. Even though the spiritual master is carrying the greatest message, the burden remains primarily with the disciple. If the disciple is scared or forced into submission, they will not be able to truly appreciate the guru's instructions.

The guru's instructions are so powerful that they remain equally as potent long after the spiritual master has left this world. This is evidenced today by the healing powers of the written instruction and recorded words of His Divine Grace A.C. Bhaktivedanta Swami Prabhupada. One of the greatest Vedic authors in history, Shrila Prabhupada started a worldwide movement dedicated to preaching the glories of Lord Krishna, Lord Chaitanya, Bhagavad-gita, and Shrimad Bhagavatam around the world. He turned Krishna into a household name. Though the swami left this world more than thirty years ago, he is still mesmerizing the pure souls who humbly submit themselves before him. Since he wrote so many books and delivered so many lectures, people can still approach him today and learn about Krishna. In fact, people today have an opportunity not available even to the swami's direct disciples back during his time on earth.

Since he was travelling around the world, opening centers and speaking to large audiences, Shrila Prabhupada's disciples didn't have the chance to associate with him on a daily basis. People today, however, can listen to his lectures every single day. His books are quite voluminous as well, for it would take an entire lifetime to read through all of them and fully grasp their meanings. For Vaishnavas, the guru is honored every day of the year, but especially on the anniversary of his appearance day. This day is known as Vyasa Puja, for the Vaishnava spiritual master is a representative of Vyasadeva, the celebrated Vedic saint, author, and direct disciple of Narada Muni.

Just as Valmiki satisfied Narada by regularly chanting Rama's name, Shrila Prabhupada and all the gurus in his line can be satisfied by our regular chanting of the maha-mantra, "Hare Krishna Hare Krishna, Krishna Krishna, Hare Hare, Hare Rama Hare Rama, Rama Rama, Hare Hare". There can be many facets to the collective discipline known as devotional service, but nothing is more effective and more recommended than the chanting of this mantra. To provide a daily routine, a guideline to ensure that chanting and hearing of God's name was performed, Prabhupada advised everyone to chant at least sixteen rounds of this mantra on a set of japa beads. Though this may take a long time to complete every day, it is the most effective process for spiritual realization in this age. We should all try to adopt this chanting regimen, if not for ourselves, then at least for the great spiritual masters who sacrificed everything for our benefit. Chanting this mantra will make them happy, and thus enable us to offer the greatest gift to the gurus that we owe so much to.

VYASA PUJA II

It is the settled conclusion of the Vedic seers that the greatest benediction in life is to have the association of saints. More specifically, if the dust coming from the lotus feet of the guru, or spiritual master, can be accepted just one time, there is no counting the number of spiritual merits, or sukriti, that follows. Just humbly submitting before any person is difficult enough, so the need for surrendering before a human being recognized for his wisdom and knowledge of spiritual matters takes many lifetimes to accept. But to those who do find the bona fide guru and bask in his association, the benefits reaped are too many to count, and the credit for the subsequent success goes directly to the spiritual master and his teachers. Since the guru can never be fully appreciated for his impact, occasions like Vyasa Puja allow for some time to reflect on the mercy of the spiritual master and what he is capable of.

A puja is a formalized worship, wherein obeisances are offered to the beneficiary of the ceremony. Vyasa refers to Vyasadeva, the literary incarnation of the Supreme Personality of Godhead, Lord Krishna. The Vedas are the oldest scriptures in existence, and since they emanate directly from Krishna and describe devotion to Him, they are considered non-different from Him. As the Vedas were originally just one work consisting of prayers and hymns, they could only be understood by the purest men. As time passes from the beginning of creation, man's ability to think critically and retain relevant pieces of information dwindles. Therefore Vyasadeva comes to divide the Vedas and write supplementary literature known as the Puranas. Vyasadeva compiled so much literature that some people refuse to believe that he even existed. Proof of his influence and divine nature is seen, however, in the behavior and glories of his disciples and their descendants. The bona fide spiritual master is one whose line of instruction is either linked to Vyasa or at least reaches the same conclusion that he put forth, that life's aim is to worship the Supreme Lord Hari, the original Personality of Godhead.

Interestingly enough, having the audience of a pure devotee is considered a greater blessing than actually meeting the Lord in person. Shri Narada Muni, the spiritual master of Vyasadeva, was blessed through good association, as was Valmiki, who was originally a dacoit. Meeting the Supreme Lord in person is certainly a terrific reward, but, at the same time, it doesn't automatically lead to one's knowing how to act and what their true nature is. The devotee, on the other hand, lives bhakti-yoga, or devotional service, therefore they are deputed by the Supreme Lord to teach others about what they have learned and how to make the most out of the human form of life.

The spirit soul is the essence of identity within any life form, but only with a human birth can the soul take the necessary steps to reacquaint itself with its true dharma, or foremost characteristic. One who takes instruction from a brahmana, or a priest devoted to real religion, earns the title of dvija, or one who is twice-born. The first birth is from the parents, but this doesn't automatically awaken the dormant God consciousness resting within the heart. The instruction provided by the spiritual master gives the second and more important birth. The rekindling of the torchlight of knowledge that is part and parcel of the soul is the more important giver of life. Since this birth comes from the guru, how can his glories ever be fully appreciated?

Since man is forgetful of his constitutional position, those who accept the instructions of the spiritual master and take them to heart will acquire tremendous skills. The guru's primary teaching is that one devote themselves to bhakti-yoga. The quintessential act of bhakti is the chanting of the holy names, "Hare Krishna Hare Krishna, Krishna Krishna, Hare Hare, Hare Rama Hare Rama, Rama Rama, Hare Hare". There are other spiritual teachers who provide different instructions, such as how to do meditational yoga, how to study Vedanta, and how to work without attachment to the results. These instructions can be beneficial, but they fail to extract the full potential for love found within the soul.

It is for this reason that the dust of the lotus feet of the devotee is considered life's greatest blessing. In the Vedic tradition there are many sacred places of pilgrimage known as tirthas. Just by visiting these places, so many benedictions are guaranteed. These spots are related to Lord Vishnu in some way or another. Vishnu is another name for Krishna which means the "all-pervading". In His Vishnu form, the Lord is opulently adorned and has four hands instead of two. The sacred pilgrimage sites are full of saints, who use the auspicious surroundings to increase the efficacy of their service. This shows how pure the Supreme Lord is. Any ordinary river is not that important, but one attached to Vishnu becomes visited by millions of people each year. Similarly, there are tons of teachers and devotees of objects not related to God, but they are not given the attention that the saints are, those who are intimately associated with Bhagavan, the Supreme Lord fully endowed with every beneficial attribute. The potential to meet saints is the real benefit of visiting a tirtha, as the relationship with Vishnu fully matures through their association.

The guru can be considered the travelling tirtha, as he brings with him the auspiciousness found in the sacred pilgrimage sites. This auspiciousness is present in every aspect of the spiritual master, including the dust that comes from his feet. The lotus feet of the guru are the cherished objects for the devotee because they symbolize the proper way to approach God. Through humility, kind submission, and service to one who is deserving of it, true enlightenment can be revealed.

What is the result of following the chanting prescriptions and the restrictions on meat eating, gambling, intoxication and illicit sex? As Krishna consciousness awakens from within, many new abilities arise. All of a sudden the person who was previously dumb, lazy, and harboring a hateful attitude can produce volumes upon volumes of literature praising their beloved Lord and His devotees. They may not even have had any formal training in writing, grammar, or composition. They may even have done poorly during their school years in these subjects. Yet simply from hearing Krishna-katha, talks about Shri Krishna, and the beauty of devotional service from the guru, the humble soul can become an expert reciter, never running out of material to share with the general public.

When someone becomes skilled in a particular field, it's not surprising that they would garner a lot of attention. The Vaishnava poets, singers and writers are the most glorified, for their fame stretches the full boundaries of time and space. Their glories know no end, and they continue to be honored and worshiped long after they physically leave the earth. The real credit for superexcellent ability in spiritual endeavors actually goes to the guru, for without his planting of the seed of the creeper of devotional service, bhakti-lata-bija, the full blown tree of transcendental ecstasy and its resultant fruits would never have manifest.

If the guru is due credit for the wonderful writings of his disciples, how can he ever be properly honored? With each new work produced the guru's fame and glory further increase. In this respect, His Divine Grace A.C. Bhaktivedanta Swami Prabhupada is worthy of endless adoration. Not only did he personally accept thousands of disciples during his time on earth, through his published works and recorded lectures he continues to rescue those swimming in the sea of nescience. So many past lives have been spoiled pursuing sense gratification, but Shrila Prabhupada doesn't hold this against anyone. His message comes directly from Krishna, so it is very powerful and can turn even the biggest fool into a genius.

An issue of contention may be raised regarding the negative traits exhibited by disciples and devotees who took instruction from a guru. If a saint deserves the credit for the wonderful qualities of his disciples, including the brilliance of their writings, shouldn't he then be blamed for their shortcomings? Though this seems logical enough, the rules don't apply equally. To explain this the example most often cited is that of fire and its production of smoke. Fire is a purifying agent, as it can disintegrate pretty much anything. Though the fire can produce smoke, which is impure, the fire itself never loses its properties. Similarly, the guru may have some errant disciples who can be compared to smoke, but this doesn't diminish his standing whatsoever.

Isn't this a cop out though? The guru gets the credit for all the good, but then gets none of the blame for the bad? How does this make any sense? Let's think of it this way: The bad qualities are always there in a person. By "bad", we refer to anything that is divorced of its relationship to God. A sinful reaction is really just the negative consequence to doing something incorrectly. Since we know that the spirit soul's original home is in the spiritual sky alongside God in His personal form, any soul who takes birth in a realm governed by reincarnation must be considered sinful. Moreover, from our present birth we know that in the past we failed to become fully God conscious by the time of death.

The Bhagavad-gita, Krishna's direct instructions offered on the battlefield of Kurukshetra some five thousand years ago, reveals that whatever state of mind we have at the time of death, that state we will attain without fail. Since our present birth is in a human form, where we are born ignorant of the Supreme Lord's divine nature and the need for worshiping Him, by rule our consciousness at the time of our previous death was not focused on God. Thus every material birth is sinful, with man having an innate tendency towards following bad habits.

The bona fide guru is thus not responsible for the sinful behavior in man. This penchant is already given to us at the time of birth, or, more accurately, it is provided to us through our wishes. The guru teaches devotional service and how to throw away attachment to sinful activity. If, after taking instruction from him, the sinful behavior continues, it should be understood that the root elements of desire for material association remained, sort of like the last flames of a raging fire that has almost been put out. If the guru doesn't teach attachment to sinful behavior, how can he be blamed for the mistakes made by his disciples?

The glories of the guru are too many to count. His presence in our lives is directly due to Krishna's intervention. Those who sincerely desire to have the Lord's association and be able to think of Him without fail will never be denied. That precious dust from the lotus feet of the spiritual master will come soon enough. No greater gift can be found in this world than the association of saints.

On this Vyasa Puja day we honor and remember one of the more notable saints in modern times, Shrila Prabhupada, who lives on forever through his recorded instructions.

VYASA PUJA III

Okay, so you have your principles. You've developed them either through experience or personal instruction offered from an authority figure. Now you're in a position of importance, so you want to imbibe the same principles in the people you can influence. But in a complex world, where your survival is dependent upon living entities who have their own dependencies, not every situation is ideal. Sometimes you have to compromise in order to get what you want, which thus pecks away at your cherished principles. With the spiritual master, however, his primary dependency is on the word of his spiritual master, who follows the same behavior, which means that the original dependency is on the Supreme Lord. This makes the Vaishnava spiritual master and his message beyond reproach, and so the guru is honored every day and especially on the occasion of Vyasa Puja.

The modern day politician is the classic example of the person who must compromise their principles. In the system of democracy, the citizens are believed to be insulated from despotism. A group of a few cannot impose their will upon everyone else. At least that is the hope with democracy, though in the present state such an imposition can take place through the will of the majority of the highest court in the land. A founding document can prohibit the government from doing something, but nothing can stop the legislature from adopting such a course. The highest court in the land is expected to uphold the principles of the founding document, but as free will is provided to every living entity, nothing is to stop members of the court from disregarding the document they are sworn to uphold and defend. For whatever reason, be it political or personal, members of the court can choose in favor of a law that strips away the very freedoms of the citizen that are supposedly guaranteed in amendments to the founding document.

The politician plays in a game where success is measured by popularity. What easier way is there to earn favor than to hand out goodies? The flaw with this method is that every person is equally a citizen. This means that granting favors to only a few is inherently unfair. That unfairness is also incongruent with trying to abide by principles in one's own life, especially as they relate to dependents. Say, for instance, that you're a politician who is also a parent. You don't want your children doing drugs, skipping school, or drinking alcohol. You may have done these things when you were young, so you know that your kids shouldn't follow the same dangerous behavior.

Your views can be compromised in this area through the accusation of hypocrisy. "Hey, you did these things when you were young, so why are you getting on my case right now?" Also, what if your child mingles with children of other politicians? What if somebody else's child introduces drugs and alcohol to the scene? What if the child's parent is a high ranking government official, someone whose favor you require in order to stay in office? Are you going to reprimand the government official, telling them to keep their delinquent child away from yours?

The Vaishnava spiritual master is in a unique position because they are dependent only upon Krishna, or God, for their livelihood. The spiritual master doesn't always live in the renounced order, but those who are in such a status are insulated that much more. Vyasa Puja celebrates the spiritual master, and its name is in honor of Vyasadeva, the literary incarnation of the Supreme Personality of Godhead. No one in history has written more than Vyasa. He wrote so much transcendental literature that some fools mistakenly think that he didn't exist. They will speculate that Vyasa was perhaps a title assigned to various speakers or that maybe he was a mythological character.

He existed in the flesh, and proof of his existence is found in the unmatched brilliance of the teachers who follow in his line. Though Vyasadeva wasn't in the renounced order, he wasn't encumbered in his teaching. The brahmana, or priestly person in the mode of goodness, accepts the responsibility to instruct others. That instruction is tailored to the recipient's qualities. Just as in a school system there are different classes for different subjects and grade levels, the word of God is shaped differently based on the mode of nature one lives in. A person in the modes of passion and ignorance may be better suited for trade and business, whereas a person mostly in passion is an ideal candidate for defending the innocent.

The brahmana is in the mode of goodness, so they live in knowledge. This knowledge is of the difference between matter and spirit. The spirit soul is the essence of identity, and the sum collection of spiritual particles is known as Brahman. Both the spiritual and material energies come from God, and the birth of the living entities takes place through the injection of the marginal potency into the external potency. This implantation is enacted by God, and the result is a seemingly infinite number of creatures who are a combination of matter and spirit.

The brahmana has the highest occupation, and the corresponding highest status of life is sannyasa, or the renounced order. This is typically the last part of one's time within a specific body, and it occurs after completion of student life. Householder life and retired married life are optional stages after the fact, but sannyasa is where one prepares to die. It is said in the Bhagavad-gita that whatever state of being one remembers at the time of death, that state they will attain without fail. Therefore one who can think of God when dying attains the highest state in the next life. Sannyasa prepares one for this remembrance.

The sannyasa order brings gravitas to the brahmana, as the message carries more weight when the person offering it is not compromised in their beliefs. The principal teaching of the brahmana sannyasi who follows in Vyasadeva's line is to always think of God. Especially in the present age of quarrel and hypocrisy, where just openly espousing a belief in God makes you a noteworthy fellow, the best way to stay true to the highest principle is to always chant the holy names, "Hare Krishna Hare Krishna, Krishna Krishna, Hare Hare, Hare Rama Hare Rama, Rama Rama, Hare Hare".

Gambling, intoxication, meat eating and illicit sex are the strongest inhibitors to the formation of the divine consciousness. Therefore the Vaishnava spiritual master strongly recommends against these activities, and since they avoid sinful behavior themselves, their message is not tainted. The ideal example in this regard is His Divine Grace A.C. Bhaktivedanta Swami Prabhupada. Who could speak anything against him? At an old age he abandoned a comfortable life in Vrindavana to preach to the world the glories of bhakti-yoga, the divine love so nicely presented by Vyasadeva in the sacred Shrimad Bhagavatam.

Bhaktivedanta Swami, also known as Shrila Prabhupada, lived bhakti-yoga day and night, and so when he taught others how to practice Krishna consciousness, his message was not compromised. Whether one person heard him or one million, there was no difference in his attitude. In full surrender to the divine, or sharanagati, the burden for success is shifted to the Supreme Lord. This means that no person can check the practice of devotion. There was no fear of compromising principles in Shrila Prabhupada because what could anyone do to him? Could they threaten to get his temples shut down? Could they try to stop his preaching? Certainly nefarious characters may have attempted such things, but the Vaishnava can practice their devotion in any situation, living under a tree if they have to.

Due to his tireless efforts, thousands of humble disciples subsequently took up the cause of devotion, and the chanting of the holy names continues on to this day, as Krishna is now a household name around the world. On the occasion of Vyasa Puja we honor that spiritual master of the world, the jagad-guru Shrila Prabhupada, who continues to spread his uncompromising message through his published works.

In Closing:

To stay true the principled person tries,
But due to dependency they must compromise.

This is the way of life, what can they do?
You scratch my back, and I'll scratch yours too.

But Vaishnava only on Krishna relies,
Can live in place small or large in size.

Whether a thousand people or just one hears,
In preaching message of bhakti there is no fear.

I honor Bhaktivedanta Swami, His divine grace,
Of compromise of principles in him not a trace.

RADHASHTAMI I

When worship of Lord Krishna is performed in a temple or any other formal gathering, the deity or picture that is offered obeisances usually contains two entities. Surely Krishna is always there, either holding His flute, dipping His hand into a butter pot, or lifting a gigantic hill. Each one of these poses represents a particular activity performed by the Lord during His time on earth. In fact, we know from the Shrimad Bhagavatam that these pastimes continue to take place all the time throughout the millions of universes in existence. At this precise moment somewhere in the universe, Lord Krishna is appearing from the womb of Mother Devaki, lifting Govardhana Hill, stealing butter and yogurt from the neighbors, and even dancing with His beloved. This eternal companion brings the greatest pleasure to the Lord and therefore she is always with Krishna in mind, body, or spirit. The devotees understand that since this divine entity represents the height of unadulterated love for God, she is equally worthy of worship. Her name is Shrimati Radharani and her appearance day is celebrated as the occasion of Radhashtami.

Normally we think of God as a singular entity. Those who believe in multiple gods are often viewed as pagans or people who make up their own religion. In fact, the very existence of multiple gods utterly contradicts the notion of a Supreme Controller. In Vedic terminology, the Supreme Lord is known by thousands of names such as Parameshvara, Bhagavan, Achyuta, and Aja. These names point to His supremacy in the areas of power, opulence, infallibility, and transcending birth. Since only one entity can possess all of these qualities at the same time, there can only be one God. If there are multiple gods, it means that more than one entity is deemed as Supreme. Therefore the concept of God loses its value.

In the Vedic tradition, there are certainly many god-like entities. They are known as devas, and they have extraordinary powers in their ability to create, maintain, and destroy in the material world. This distinction between material and spiritual worlds is what separates the devas from the devah-varah, or chief divine entity.

The chief is known by the name of Krishna and He is the original form of Godhead. Due to His kind mercy, this singular divine entity is known by other forms and expansions such as Vishnu, Rama, Narasimha, Vamana, and Chaitanya. These forms are non-different from the original, so they are equally as worshipable as Krishna Himself.

Yet there are also separated entities which are not exactly direct expansions of the Lord, but which are still treated on the same level. The Vedas inform us that Krishna, or God, is the energetic. The living entities, separated expansions of the Supreme Lord, serve as Krishna's energy. Since these expansions are separated, they are not equally as potent as the original. In this way, the living entities, we human beings and other forms of life, are similar to God in quality, but vastly inferior in quantitative powers. Krishna is the reservoir of energy, and as tiny sparks emanating from the gigantic fire, we are meant to be in association with that powerhouse of energy. When the energy becomes separated from the energetic in terms of consciousness, the energy becomes subject to delusion, bewilderment, and the loss of intelligence. The greatest delusion, the nadir of material existence, arises when the energy thinks itself to be the energetic. This is represented by the idea of "I am God" or "I am Brahman", with Brahman taken to be the ultimate feature of the divine. This is the mindset adopted by the class of transcendentalists known as Mayavadis or impersonalists.

The living entities, as Krishna's energy, are certainly equal parts of the transcendental effulgence known as Brahman. At the same time, they can never be an on equal footing with the Lord. In order to realize one's true relationship to the Supreme Energetic, one must see past the effulgence of Brahman and stare directly at the transcendental, blissful, and sweet form of the Lord. Those who are able to do so achieve a heightened state of consciousness, a mindset where they are always thinking of Krishna in various moods of love. Those who are at the highest level of transcendental love are thus considered the representation of the perfected energy of the Lord. The one entity who best embodies this mindset of Krishna consciousness is, not surprisingly, Krishna's eternal consort, Shrimati Radharani.

Radharani, often referred to as Radha, is more than just God's wife. They say that the wife is the better half of man, meaning she is the energy behind the husband. Behind every great man is a powerful woman, someone who stands by her man and makes sure he is always acting properly and is well cared for. This woman is usually either the mother or the wife. The terms "husband" and "wife" refer to the system of marriage, something which involves rules, regulations, and dharma, or occupational duty. Certainly other non-different forms of Godhead take one or many different spouses, but with Krishna's case, His relationship with Radha is much greater than that shared between a husband and a wife. With Radha and Krishna, there are no rules. There are no occupational duties or regulations guiding their relationship. Krishna is always with Radha and Radha is always with Krishna. In this way, they are equal. They represent the fusion of the energy and the energetic, the most powerful synergistic relationship.

Shrimati Radharani's love and devotion towards Krishna is so strong that she even takes to chastising Him on certain occasions. Normally taking to criticism is an act of the miser, someone who is outside the bonds of affection. Love and devotion usually equates to forgiveness and the overlooking of short-comings. Yet with Radharani, her love for Krishna is so strong that even her acts of criticizing are considered praiseworthy. An example of this was seen when Krishna's cousin Uddhava once visited Vrindavana. When Lord Krishna advented on this earth five thousand years ago, He spent His childhood years in a village called Vrindavana. This town still exists in India and is actually a replica of the same realm that can be found in the spiritual world. Krishna grew up in a family of cowherds, so all the neighbors were involved in similar occupations. At night, Krishna would engage in romantic escapades with Radha and the other neighboring cowherd girls known as the gopis. Unscrupulous commentators and non-devotees will never be able to understand these intimate dealings, for they transgress all the rules and mores of society. This is the beauty of the relationship between Radha and Krishna. The divine couple is the object of piety and virtue. One who takes to the path of righteousness but doesn't eventually come to the stage of loving God has essentially wasted their time.

As with any other activity in this world, Krishna's dealings with the gopis and Radha had to come to an end eventually. As He grew up, Krishna had other affairs to tend to in neighboring towns such as Mathura and Dvaraka. The day He left Vrindavana was a very sad one for all the residents, but especially so for the gopis. They cried and cried and couldn't understand why their beloved Krishna was leaving them. Shortly after His departure, Krishna sent His dear friend and cousin Uddhava to relay some information to the residents of Vrindavana, and especially the gopis, all of whom were suffering greatly in Krishna's absence.

Uddhava was almost identical to Krishna in appearance, so when he first approached the gopis, they thought that maybe he was Krishna. But upon closer examination, they could tell that he wasn't. Shrimati Radharani wasn't really interested in Uddhava's words, for she was still upset with Krishna for leaving them. The gopis took Uddhava to the forest since they knew he had a message for them from Krishna. Radharani, who was quite upset, stepped away from the group and began talking to a bumblebee that was buzzing around her. Radha thought maybe the bee was sent by Krishna to deliver a message. Thus she took the opportunity to let the bumblebee know just what she was feeling towards her prana-natha, or the Lord of her life, Krishna.

Radha took to criticizing Krishna, telling the bumblebee that the Lord was not very reliable, nor was He very righteous. She said that the Lord had enjoyed with the gopis intimately in the forest and then abruptly left to go live as a king in Mathura. She essentially compared Him to a person who takes advantage of a woman and then leaves her without protection. She then continued with her criticisms by referencing activities performed by Krishna's previous incarnations. The Sanskrit term avatara refers to one who descends, thus it deals solely with Krishna or Vishnu. The Vedas tell us that as many waves as there are in the ocean are how many avataras of Vishnu exist. Nevertheless, the list of the primary avataras is mentioned in books like the Shrimad Bhagavatam. Radha made reference to incidents pertaining to some of these incarnations.

Shrimati Radharani criticized several activities performed by Krishna's previous incarnation of Lord Ramachandra. In the Treta Yuga, Lord Vishnu appeared on earth in the guise of a valiant warrior prince named Rama, a descendant of the Raghu dynasty. On one occasion, the Lord was residing in the forest of Dandaka with His wife Sita Devi and younger brother Lakshmana. A Rakshasi, a female demon, came and propositioned Rama. According to the etiquette established for the warrior caste, a prince should never refuse the advances of a woman. A warrior is to provide protection after all, so if a woman wants to enjoy conjugal love, the warrior is essentially tasked with providing that love and giving protection at the same time. Lord Rama, however, loved Sita, who ironically was the same Radharani, very much, so He refused Shurpanakha's advances. He jokingly said that Lakshmana wasn't married and that she should cavort with him instead. Not heeding His advice, Shurpanakha dashed at Sita in hopes of eliminating the competition. Lakshmana couldn't stand for this, so he immediately stepped in and disfigured the female demon. Her nose having been cut off, she ran home to tell her brother, the King of Lanka, Ravana. Radharani mentions this incident to support her claim that Krishna has always been an enemy to the rules of propriety, for He allowed an innocent woman to be disfigured because of His love for Sita.

Radharani wasn't finished talking to the bumblebee. She next mentioned another incident from Lord Rama's life, where He killed a monkey king named Vali. After Shurpanakha went crying to Ravana, the demon devised a plan where he was able to kidnap Sita and take her back to his kingdom. In His subsequent search for His missing wife, Rama ended up forming an alliance with a monkey king named Sugriva. Vali was Sugriva's brother, and the two were mortal enemies due to a dispute over the right to rule a kingdom. Lord Rama agreed to help Sugriva defeat Vali and regain his kingdom. Yet the nature of Vali's defeat and death weren't exactly ideal. Since Vali was stronger, there was no way for Sugriva to defeat him. Lord Rama devised a plan where Sugriva would first engage Vali in battle, leaving the door open for Rama to attack. This is precisely what would happen, as Rama would shoot and kill Vali from behind while the monkey was engaged in a fight with his brother. According to the rules of fighting established for the kshatriya order, an enemy is never to be attacked while he is engaged in a fair fight with the opposition. Yet since Rama was God Himself, such rules and regulations never apply to Him. In fact, if one is devoted to the Lord in thought, word, and deed, the Lord will take whatever action is needed to secure the devotee's happiness. This also explains Krishna's dealings with the gopis. As pure lovers of God, the gopis wanted association with Krishna and nothing else. Though they weren't His wives or even unmarried girls, the Lord enjoyed with them simply to satisfy their pure desires. Nevertheless, Radharani mentioned Rama's killing of Vali as another example of Krishna's impious nature.

So it may seem strange that Radharani is worthy of worship even though she openly takes to criticizing Krishna from time to time. But in reality, such displays of emotion are mere symptoms of pure love for God. Being a surrendered soul means you always think of and rely on Krishna no matter what, through the good times and the bad. After speaking this way about Krishna to the bumblebee, Radharani immediately lamented and was hoping that the bumblebee wouldn't tell Krishna what she had said. The reality of the situation was that she was completely devoted to Krishna, so through feelings of separation, she took to criticizing Him. Only the devotees can criticize the Lord in this way. Others, who are competing with God for the title of greatest enjoyer, can never take issue with the Lord and still be considered pure and worthy of worship. Only the greatest devotees, those who worship in separation, can be worthy of love and adoration for their behavior.

What is the difference between worship in separation and worship in person? Worship of Krishna in separation is considered superior because it is more conducive towards Krishna consciousness. There are other famous expressions such as "don't know what you've got til it's gone" and "absence makes the heart grow fonder" which convey a similar message. When this separation is applied to spiritual life, it evokes a certain type of bliss which is unmatched. When appearing on earth, Shrimati Radharani and her various expansions deal with great separation from the Lord precisely to taste the bliss that arises from separation. Sita Devi also spent much time away from Lord Rama.

Goswami Tulsidas, the great devotee of Lord Rama, remarks in his poetry that he hopes to be just like the Chatak bird. This bird is known for staring at the dark blue raincloud, a cloud which has the exact same complexion as Rama's [Krishna/Vishnu] body. Yet Tulsidas also prays that no matter how long this bird looks at the cloud, it is better for it not to rain, for if it did, then the bird would maybe become lax in its devotion and love for the cloud. In this way, the great poet is asking to always worship Rama in separation, for that evokes the greatest transcendental love and maintains the firm link in consciousness between the devotee and the Divine. Tulsidas asks that even if the bird dies, one should not turn its beak away from the raincloud during the performance of the last rites. In the Vedic tradition, last rites are usually performed in the sacred Ganges River so as to facilitate the liberation of the departed from the cycle of birth and death. In this way, the great saint tells us that worship of God in His personal, original form through love and devotion is far superior to any other reward, including that of liberation.

This worship in separation is seen in perfected form with Shrimati Radharani. In fact, Lord Krishna was so enamored by Radha's devotion to Him that He decided to appear on earth in a dual incarnation of Radha-Krishna to see exactly what this devotion was like. Appearing as Shri Krishna Chaitanya some five hundred years ago, the Lord played the role of a devotee of Krishna, experiencing many of the same separation pains felt by Radha. Lord Chaitanya taught us by example to always remain attached to the Supreme Lord and His pleasure potency in a mood of loving separation. This mood can be adopted through the chanting of the holy names of God, "Hare Krishna Hare Krishna, Krishna Krishna, Hare Hare, Hare Rama Hare Rama, Rama Rama, Hare Hare". Therefore we should all hang on to this most sacred of mantras as our lifeline. On Radhashtami Day, we celebrate the greatest devotee of Krishna, Shrimati Radharani. As much as she loves Krishna, she does not keep Him to herself. She is so kind that she allows others to also taste the sweet transcendental mellows of bhakti. Worship of Radha is as good as worship of Krishna, therefore the two are always seen together for the pure-hearted to love and adore.

RADHASHTAMI II

Radhashtami is the anniversary of the appearance day of Shrimati Radharani, the eternal consort of Lord Krishna, the Supreme Personality of Godhead. The thrill felt by lovers courting one another, playing jokes and enjoying each other's company, is found in its purified form in the intimate dealings between Radha and Krishna. To understand the transcendental nature of their interactions and derive the full benefit from hearing about them, one must be very fortunate. Without a properly situated consciousness, the conditioned mind will take Radha and Krishna's interactions to be similar to the boyfriend and girlfriend dealings we are accustomed to seeing. Yet, just like the expensive antiques in the living room of the house, the pastimes between Radha and Krishna are meant to be enjoyed by those who understand its value. Put the priceless vase in the hands of children and they are liable to break it, not understanding its importance. With the benediction of wonderful holidays like Radhashtami on the Vaishnava calendar, any person can become familiar with Shrimati Radharani and her important position as Krishna's most beloved.

If you are God and you have someone who makes you extremely happy, it would make sense that your devotees would love her very much as well. We can just imagine the divine character of that pleasure-giving person, how many wonderful qualities they have. The Shri Chaitanya Charitamrita of Krishnadasa Kaviraja Gosvami lists some of Radharani's most important qualities. She appeared on this earth as the daughter of King Vrishabhanu and Mother Kirtida. The exact sequence of events relating to her appearance can vary by creation. The variations found in Vedic literature do not give evidence to the theory that the information is just mythology or hyped up stories. On the contrary, as the creation and destruction of the earth and other material planets go through repeating cycles, the exact sequence of events pertaining to the pastimes of Lord Krishna and His associates isn't always the same.

This also reveals why there are sometimes variations in the telling of the Ramayana, which describes the life and pastimes of

Lord Rama, one of Krishna's most famous incarnations. Indeed, even Goswami Tulsidas, who is sometimes criticized for having differences in his Ramacharitamanasa, provides a few different details in his other shorter poem on the same subject matter called the Gitavali. Was he not aware that he contradicted himself? Was he not aware that his versions of the events of Rama's life differed slightly from what was found in the original Ramayana composed by Maharishi Valmiki? Obviously not, as the Lord doesn't follow exactly the same behavior every single day. Just as our day is measured by the movement of the sun, the length of the creation is equated to one day of Lord Brahma, who is the creator. In each day of Brahma, there are cycles of the different yugas, with the sun that is Krishna appearing at similar times in each cycle. Though the spiritual sun that is Krishna doesn't always follow the same path through the sky, the majority of the events relating to His pastimes occurs at similar times and follows similar patterns.

With Shrimati Radharani's appearance, the earth was graced with the lotus feet of Krishna's beloved. Around five thousand years ago the two roamed the sacred land of Vrajabhumi, performing wonderful pastimes together, many of which are documented in the Shrimad Bhagavatam, the crown jewel of Vedic literature. That the heartwarming tale of Radha and Krishna is included in this sacred work is enough to give it superior status. Though Vedic literature is quite vast and comprehensive, one needn't study every single scriptural work to find full enlightenment. Rather, just lending an ear to the Bhagavatam and having an open mind when learning about Krishna, His beauty, His pastimes and the glories of His associates are enough to attain all the knowledge necessary in life.

Even if one isn't given to hearing about Krishna, by visiting a place of pilgrimage, a tirtha, and taking bath in its sacred waters so many sins accumulated over many past lifetimes in the material world can be washed away. The soul is eternal, but the bodies it occupies are not. Just as our clothes get worn out and dirty over time, the dwellings occupied by the soul undergo development and decay. The sins accumulated are rooted in desire, with the consciousness not wanting to return to its constitutional position of pure loving devotion to the Supreme Lord. The inkling towards love is always there; but in the absence of bhakti, or pure devotion, it manifests in so many other forms. Only in bhakti-yoga, or devotional service, does the loving propensity find a tangible outlet, a recipient who can never be smothered, a person who will never scorn the lover, a person who will instead find ways to increase the devotee's attachment.

One of the most famous tirthas for devotees of Krishna is Radha-kunda. Adjacent to this is Shyama-kunda. These are the famous ponds dear to Radha and Krishna, and the story of how they came about is quite heartwarming. When Krishna appeared in Mathura in the prison cell of King Kamsa, He was immediately transferred to the neighboring farm community of Vrindavana, where He would be safe from the king's wicked plots. A prophecy had warned Kamsa that his sister Devaki's eighth son would kill him. Not taking any chances, the king locked up his sister and her husband Vasudeva in prison. With each son they produced, Kamsa came and threw the infant against a stone wall. He was anxiously awaiting Devaki's eighth son to appear so that he could keep the tradition going.

Lord Krishna had arranged everything perfectly, so the prophecy was real and could not be reversed. Krishna decided to grow up in Vrindavana, though, to grace the residents there with His presence, for His childhood form and activities are the most attractive. Just imagine how much joy we get from watching our young sons, daughters, nieces, nephews and grandchildren play around the house and try to learn to walk and talk. Add the Supreme Personality of Godhead and His immediate expansion Lord Balarama to the mix, and what you get is the unmatched pleasure felt by the residents of Vrajabhumi.

To increase the transcendental satisfaction felt, there were many episodes involving danger, with Krishna able to save the day every time. Kamsa found out that Devaki's child had made it to Vrindavana, so he sent demon after demon there to try to kill Him. One took the form of a bull and was named Arishtasura. He was killed easily by Krishna, but the Lord's gopi friends were a little concerned with the manner of the slaying. The cowherd girls of the town were especially devoted to Krishna. Among the gopis, Shrimati Radharani was the chief, as she enjoyed Krishna's company the most and had captured His heart.

A unique aspect of the mood of devotion practiced by the gopis is that they fly pass the stage of having reverence for God. For celebrity athletes and movie stars, it's nice having adoring fans, but having peers and equals is more enjoyable because they allow for the exchanges of emotion to be more real. In devotional service, the transcendental mellows followed by the gopis are the topmost because they are more intimate than the reverential spirit usually reserved for God, who is the supreme powerful. It is not that one should just casually address Krishna and treat Him as an equal without cause. Rather, when the love is so strong, the attachment will be there no matter what, so there is no need to fear Krishna's punishments, for He is like the dearest family member.

After Krishna killed the bull demon, the gopis were concerned that His sin of killing a bull would spread to the rest of the residents. Therefore they started thinking of a way to become absolved of this sin. While they were walking about, they ran into Shri Krishna, who was very happy about having saved the town from Arishtasura. When they saw Him, the gopis immediately chided Him. Shrimati Radharani told Him to stay away because He was contaminated by sin. Can we imagine saying such a thing? Krishna is the embodiment of purity. Sin only gets introduced when one is not tied to Krishna. The root cause of the material creation is forgetfulness of God, which thus forms the original sin. Since Krishna is the object of worship, He is incapable of behaving impiously.

The sentiments from Radharani were rooted in the most heartfelt emotions though. These sorts of insults gave great pleasure to Krishna, as it allowed Him to fire back with His own witty retorts. He told Radha that what He had killed was not actually a bull, but a demon in the guise of a bull. Therefore there could not be any sin attached to the demon's slaying. Radharani, ever the wise Vedic scholar, quickly responded by referencing King Indra's slaying of

Vritrasura. Vritrasura was also a demon, but by birth he was a brahmana. Therefore Indra, the king of heaven, had to suffer the sin of having killed a brahmana, which is actually one of the most grievous transgressions one can make.

Radharani thus won this short, playful debate. When Krishna wanted to know how He could become absolved of the "sin", Radha informed Him that He had to take a bath in all the sacred rivers. At this point Krishna gave up His fake humility and scoffed at her suggestion. Why would He need to visit any holy places? He is the Supreme Lord after all, so He can bring the sacred waters of the world to wherever He goes. Kicking the ground, the Lord was able to make a small ditch that soon filled up with Ganga water. Then the most sacred tirtha waters from around the world poured into the hole as well. Krishna then took His bath in front of the gopis, as if to show them He was now pure. After Radha downplayed this by saying that it was simply a display of Krishna's illusion, to remove any doubt, the Lord then summoned the sacred rivers to reveal themselves.

As the pastimes of Radha and Krishna completely delight the mind, it's not surprising what happened next. Rather than accept that Krishna had now been purified and agree to His invitation to enter His newly created pond, Radha and the gopis claimed that the water had become contaminated by Krishna's sins. Therefore if they were to step into His kunda, or pond, they would be infected with His sin. Radha then saw a hole in the ground nearby which had been created by the hoof print of Arishtasura. Taking her bangles, she started digging her own hole to be used as a bathing place. The many gopis that were there followed suit by using their bangles for digging as well. After the hole was made, they needed to fill it with water. The gopis were ready to travel far and wide to bring water from all the sacred places. Seeing their steady resolve, Krishna Himself summoned the same sacred rivers to come and fill Radha's ditch.

With her kunda now built, Shri Krishna used His flute to break the dam separating the two ponds. The Lord then took a swim in the new Radha-kunda and declared its water to be sacred. These two bathing places still exist in Vrindavana, and devotees take tremendous delight in bathing in them, as there are tremendous spiritual merits accumulated from contact with these waters. Just as Radha is dear to Krishna, so is her bathing place of Radha-kunda. And Shyama-kunda is right next to it, so just by mentally taking a dip in both waters one can keep the image of Shri Shri Radha and Krishna in their minds for a long time. The aim of human life is to always remember the Lord and His dearmost associates. Among the devotees, none are dearer to Krishna than the gopis. And among the gopis, Shrimati Radharani is the best, for she gives so much pleasure to Krishna that He is fully surrendered to her. On Radhashtami we remember Krishna's beloved, and we pray that she may have mercy on us and give us the boon of Krishna-bhakti, so that we may never forget the divine pastimes of Kishora-kishori and their sacred land of Vrajabhumi.

In Closing:

Shrimati Radharani to Krishna is most dear,
Her pastimes with the Lord pleasing to the ear.

On her appearance day her divine nature we remember,
Krishna's spiritual senses enthralled just by seeing her.

One time after killing bull demon did Krishna walk,
On the way He saw the gopis, with whom did He talk.

Radha chastised Him, saying He was now contaminated,
For killing a bull, injunction of shastras He had violated.

"In holy waters Your body You must dip,
To become free of the sin, to tirthas take a trip."

Instead, Shri Krishna made a hole in the ground with His heel,
Filling it with sacred waters, thrill of victory did He feel.

But Radha was not impressed, hoof print of Arishtasura she found,

Using their bangles to dig, by gopis large hole was made in the ground.

Krishna then summoned sacred rivers to fill Radha's kunda,
New pond was loved by Him, found next to His Shyama-kunda.

On Radhashtami we remember Radharani and her beloved pond,
Of hearing of her love for Shri Krishna we are forever fond.

RADHASHTAMI III

In bhakti-yoga there is no prerequisite of a specific ability or social status. This is in contrast to other kinds of yoga. Intelligence is required in jnana-yoga, renunciation and peace in meditational yoga, and the ability to perform a specific kind of work in karma-yoga. Yet in any social status, at any age, and in any circumstance one can be connected to the Supreme Lord in a mood of love. Love is the universal language, and so it is never bound to a specific condition. Divine love exists to the highest degree in Shrimati Radharani, and so the anniversary of her appearance day is celebrated with great pomp by Vaishnavas, to whom she is very dear.

Radharani's good qualities are too many to count and their magnitude so high that measurements don't exist to accurately describe them. She is God's pleasure potency, known as the hladini-shakti. There is the original God and then there is His energy. We are also part of His energy, and being technically part of the marginal aspect we have a choice in masters. Just as the free woman has a choice in suitors, the living entity can choose in favor of either material nature or the divine energy. Material nature has an illusory effect, so whatever it reveals to influence the individual soul's choice is not what it seems. On the other hand, the divine energy is the truth; it is real. The individual's true calling is association with the divine energy.

As the embodiment of the devotional attitude, Radharani never chooses in favor of the material energy. Instead, she uses her abilities to please the Supreme Lord in His original standing as Shri Krishna, the beautiful youth with a blackish complexion. He holds a flute in His hands, wears a peacock feather in His hair, and sports an enchanting smile that never leaves His face. These attributes combine to make a vision that never changes, meaning that service to it as a means of worship can take place at any time.

In exercising her choice to give pleasure to Krishna, Radha engages with her beloved in amorous sports. There is a sportive tendency within the divine, and when acting on that tendency there is the ideal playing field that is Vrindavana-dhama. The pleasure groves of that sacred land is where Radha and Krishna play, where they derive tremendous enjoyment from each other's company. The contact is so blissful that anticipation of it is considered more enjoyable than the actual meeting.

In Vrindavana, Radha offers service to Krishna in other ways as well. As a beautiful young woman, one of her skills is cooking. She was once blessed by the famous Durvasa Muni that whatever she would cook would taste like sweet nectar. Cooking is an art form, and some are naturally very talented in it. They know how to combine ingredients in such a way that tasty dishes result. They have the patience and the creativity to make preparations that everyone will enjoy.

Radha has this ability in full and she offers it as a sacrifice to her beloved. Krishna's foster mother in Vrindavana, Yashoda, calls Radharani over to cook for her boy, for she knows that He enjoys her preparations the most. Yashoda is a coordinator in this way, taking the knowledge of Radharani's culinary abilities and steering them in the right direction. Another one of Radharani's qualities is shyness, so she is not always so willing to openly show her love for Krishna. To cook for Him is a subtle way to offer service, and rather than volunteer right away, she waits until Yashoda calls upon her. This way it doesn't appear to others that she is openly desirous of pleasing Krishna, a subtlety which actually makes her love more endearing to Yashoda's son.

In bhakti-yoga, one can use whatever abilities they have to please the Lord. Cooking can be done for Krishna's pleasure by offering preparations first to the Vaishnava spiritual master, who then passes the offering up the chain of spiritual masters until it eventually reaches Krishna. Radha is the topmost servant, so if she sees sincerity in devotional service, she recommends the devotee to Krishna. And her favor is very easy to win, as she is tenderhearted by nature. Therefore followers of bhakti-yoga always pray for Radharani's blessings, and with great pomp they celebrate occasions relating to her.

Radha uses all of her qualities for Krishna's pleasure, and so one can use any of their skills to remain connected to the divine. Some are skilled in writing and others in talking. Some are naturally people-friendly, while others work better in seclusion. Something as simple as attending a gathering of devotees celebrating Shri Krishna is a way to offer service, as we influence people more with our example than with our words.

On Radhashtami we celebrate the occasion when Krishna's dearly beloved appeared on this earth to delight Him with her pastimes. She is not specifically qualified in Vedanta, nor does she sit quietly in meditation. Instead, she sacrifices all of her time, dedicates every ability and quality that she possesses, for the Supreme Lord's pleasure. She sets the perfect example in this regard, and she shows that bhakti-yoga cannot be checked by any condition. Devotion offered to her is as good as worshiping Krishna, and so the truly wise saints chant the names of both the energetic and the energy found in the maha-mantra, "Hare Krishna Hare Krishna, Krishna Krishna, Hare Hare, Hare Rama Hare Rama, Rama Rama, Hare Hare".

In Closing:

In favor of devotion she chooses,
All of her abilities she uses,
For Krishna's pleasure to see,
So that happy both will be.

From Durvasa blessing in cooking she takes,
So nectarean food for Krishna she makes.

On this blessed Radhashtami day,
Name of Krishna's beloved let me say.

DUSSEHRA I

"The mighty Rama, who possessed extraordinary strength, consecrating in accordance with the mantras prescribed in the Vedas, taking that great arrow – which was capable of removing the fears of the entire world and the Ikshvaku dynasty, capable of taking away the glory of His enemies, and conducive to His own happiness – fixed it on His bow."
(Valmiki Ramayana, Yuddha Kand, Sec 108.13-14)

Screams of joy, panic, happiness, fear, chaos, and despair are heard at different times depending on the circumstances. These sounds are indications of particular events, the results of extreme outcomes, both good and bad. There was one set of screams in particular which was so pure and indicative of the highest gain that it resounded throughout the three worlds. These screams were in response to the greatest triumph, a victory which didn't always seem possible. This victory came after great effort, and thus the resulting joy was of the topmost variety. This triumph brought so much elation that it has since been celebrated annually as the occasion of Dussehra.

Dussehra, which is also known as Rama Vijayotsava and Rama Vijay Dashami, celebrates the victory of Lord Rama, the Supreme Personality of Godhead, over Ravana, the ten-headed demon king of Lanka. Many thousands of years ago, when celestials and the strongest of demons roamed the earth, there was a great disturbance caused by Ravana. He was born a Rakshasa due to a curse imprecated on his mother by the sage Vishrava. Ravana was born with a ghoulish figure possessing ten heads. Yet it was not until he was coaxed into performing great austerities to please Lord Brahma, the grandsire and first created living entity, that he was endowed with tremendous fighting abilities. Brahma can grant any boon to any person, up to the point of immortality. Ravana asked that he be immune in battle from any celestial figure. The boon being granted, the demon immediately embarked on his world destruction tour.

The influence of the demon became so strong that the demigods eventually petitioned Lord Vishnu, the supremely opulent form of the original Godhead, to alleviate the situation. Vishnu, who is neutral in the affairs of the living entities who reside in the material world, decided to show His favoritism towards the demigods since they had asked Him very nicely. The demigods weren't asking for any personal benedictions. They simply wanted a return to their peaceful condition so that they could continue their devotional efforts. Ravana was especially keen on attacking and killing the innocent priestly class on earth. The material world can be thought of as a giant playing field where the players are ignorant of the temporary and destructible nature of the field. Since the players are enamored by the pursuit of that which is not God, or maya, they continue to play the game without stop. Since the end-goal of such play is temporary, illusive, and not related to Him, the Supreme Lord plays no direct role. Though He is certainly responsible for creating the field and empowering the governing agent known as maya, the Supreme Lord still has no interest in the temporary gains and setbacks of the players involved.

Lord Vishnu does make an exception for those intelligent living entities who have had enough of playing the game. During the Treta Yuga, these humble individuals, the sages and brahmanas, decided to use the playing surface to favor their development of Krishna consciousness, a mindset which is natural to the soul and conducive to the highest gain. The material world is full of temporary gains such as money, sex life, and good food, in addition to negative side effects such as birth, death, old age, and disease. The sages look for the highest gain: the eternal association of the Supreme Spirit, Lord Shri Krishna. Vishnu and Krishna are the same person, for all that differs is Their appearance. When the devotional efforts of those seeking the highest gain are interrupted, the Supreme Lord most certainly takes an interest.

Deciding to help the demigods deal with Ravana, the Lord descended to earth as a kshatriya prince named Rama. Lord Brahma's boons to Ravana never mentioned human beings as being part of the exempt list. Therefore Lord Vishnu cleverly found a loophole to the great powers possessed by Ravana. One may ask why the Lord would need to find roundabout ways to kill Ravana when, as God Himself, He easily could destroy anyone. The answer is that Lord Brahma is one of the most respected living entities. The demigods are elevated personalities possessing extraordinary powers which are to be used for the common good. Lord Brahma is given charge of creation; all living entities can trace their lineage to him. Lord Brahma's reward for carrying out Vishnu's orders is that he can grant any boon to any person, up to the point of liberation. Only Lord Vishnu, whose many names include Mukunda, can grant mukti, or liberation.

In order for Vishnu's empowerment of Brahma to mean something, the boons given out by Brahma cannot be checked in any way. Vishnu will never give someone a particular power and then take it back later on if He sees that it is not used properly. In Ravana's case, it appeared that Brahma's powers were being used improperly. Instead of interfering with Brahma's business, the Lord decided to work around the issue and appear on the scene Himself to kill Ravana. This would serve the purposes of pleasing the demigods, keeping Brahma's name in good standing, and providing activities for devotees to hear about and relish for generations to come.

Lord Rama assumed the most innocent of guises. He always donned a pleasing smile, and He was kind to everyone He encountered. He was a warrior after all, but this didn't take away from His compassionate nature. On many occasions in His youth, He protected the saints from the attacks of the Rakshasa demons. In order to take on Ravana in battle, Rama needed an excuse. As a pious prince, the Lord would never attack anyone without just cause. The excuse He needed came in the form of the kidnapping of Sita Devi, Rama's wife. Taken back to the island kingdom of Lanka, Sita found herself in a precarious situation, left to wonder whether her husband would ever come to rescue her. Eventually Rama made His way to Lanka with His army of monkeys headed by Sugriva and Hanuman. Lakshmana, Rama's faithful younger brother, also accompanied the party. This unconventional alliance was forged in the forest of Kishkindha, the place where Rama and Lakshmana initially made their way to after Sita's abduction.

A great war ensued between Ravana's forces and the monkeys of Rama's army. Finally, after days of fighting and many casualties, Rama and Ravana met face to face on the battlefield. This was set to be a tremendous fight, for no one had ever defeated either party. Many of the monkeys and Rakshasas stopped their fighting simply to watch the beautiful battle. The celestials and the sages were on hand to offer their kind words and prayers for Shri Rama. After seven consecutive nights of fighting, it appeared that there was no end in sight. Rama kept firing His arrows - the same arrows which had previously defeated great fighters such as Khara, Dushana, and Vali - but they weren't making a dent on Ravana. The demon, for his part, threw everything he had at Rama, and yet the Lord, who appeared as an ordinary human, simply kept smiling and shooting His serpent-like arrows.

It should be noted that the exact sequence of events varies depending on the particular kalpa. The Vedas, the ancient scriptures of India, tell us that the world is created and destroyed in repeating cycles. In each creation, the Lord appears on earth through His various incarnations and performs similar activities. Though the names of the incarnations remain the same, the exact sequence of activities can change depending on time and circumstance. Therefore the fight between Ravana and Rama concludes somewhat differently in each kalpa. In the original Ramayana authored by Maharishi Valmiki, the fight ends in the following way: After seeing that Ravana wasn't being killed by the arrows shot from His bow, Rama became a little stupefied. Ravana had ten heads, and though Rama was able to sever them from his body by use of His arrows, new heads would grow immediately. At this time, Matali, the charioteer of Shri Rama, stepped in to offer some sound words of advice. He asked Rama the rhetorical question of why He had decided to play with Ravana in this way and not destroy Him outright. Matali said that the time for Ravana's destruction had come, meaning it was time for Rama to release His most powerful weapon.

This weapon was an arrow conferred upon Rama by Agastya Rishi. There are particular sages who are very famous in the Vedic tradition, and Agastya is one of them. Krishna is known as brahmanya-devaya, meaning He is the deva, or god, of choice for the brahmanas, the priestly class of men. This speaks to the truth that there are different forms of Godhead, some of which aren't as powerful as others. The demigods are also considered expansions of the Lord, but they are not direct expansions. Different classes of men can take to worshipping different forms of the Divine, but the brahmanas prefer worship of Krishna, Vishnu, or one of their non-different expansions. Agastya Rishi is especially fond of Lord Rama, as is Rama of him.

This arrow given by Agastya Rishi was actually created by Lord Brahma. The grandsire had originally given it to Lord Indra, the chief of the demigods in the heavenly planets. Therefore this arrow was particularly powerful and destructive. Lord Rama set it to His bow, softly chanted mantras invoking its power, and set it free. Mantras are the mechanism of deliverance for followers of the Vedic tradition. A mantra is simply a sound vibration which delivers the mind. Not all mantras are the same, and Lord Rama certainly doesn't need a sound vibration to kill anyone. Yet once again, to show His great respect for His great devotee Brahma, the Lord invoked the mantra so as to empower the arrow. Once released, this arrow appeared like no other. It is described as being like an all-powerful sun, thunderbolt, and flaming serpent all wrapped into one. When this arrow pierced Ravana's chest, the demon was immediately killed. The arrow returning to Rama's quiver, the celestials, sages, and monkey-host let out a tremendous roar.

This roar was an exultation signaling victory. We sometimes see similar displays of emotion when an athlete wins a game or match, or when a person becomes freed from a terrifying condition. The screams let out by the monkeys were the most beautiful because they were indicative of their tremendous love for Rama. They weren't just happy that Ravana was killed. They were elated that the sweet, kind, and benevolent Lord had emerged victorious and would thus soon be reunited with His wife. Lakshmana, Sugriva, and Vibhishana, the commanding generals for Rama's side, welcomed the Lord, the victor of the greatest battle of all-time.

After the defeat of Ravana, all the Rakshasas fighting for his side immediately fled. Where there is victory of the Lord, there can be no evil element. The power of the demons pales in comparison to the power of the devotees. The good guys, the adherents to the wishes of the Supreme Lord, need to be encouraged and given hope every now and then. With Rama's victory, the monkeys felt like they were invincible. Their terrible screams reminded the enemy that there was no chance of victory.

In the dark age of Kali that we currently live in, the non-devotees seem to have a great influence on the workings of society. By remembering Rama's victory over Ravana and the screams of the monkeys fighting for the Lord's side, we can be bucked up in our battle against the unwanted forces of this world. Just as the victorious screams of the monkeys signaled the fleeing of the Rakshasas from the battlefield, the constant chanting of the holy names of the Lord, "Hare Krishna Hare Krishna, Krishna Krishna, Hare Hare, Hare Rama Hare Rama, Rama Rama, Hare Hare", will mark the retreat of all unwanted spirits and elements from our lives. Giving succor and strength to the warrior-like devotees of the Lord, this mantra proves to be the fuel of the engine of devotion. Darkness can never survive where there is light. The demons can never survive where the presence of God is strong. The presence of the Lord is strongest where His names are constantly heard and glorified. On Dussehra day, we remember the benevolent Lord Rama, the beautiful arrow shot from His bow that killed Ravana, and the wonderful screams of joy shouted by the devotees on the battlefield.

DUSSEHRA II

sa tu nihataripuh sthirapratijñaḥ |
svajanabalābhivṛto raṇe rarāja |
raghukulanṛpanandano mahujā |
stridaśagaṇairabhisaṃvṛto yathendraḥ | |

"That Rama, the delight of the king of the Raghu dynasty, who had just slayed his enemy and was thus steady in His vow, possessing tremendous might, shone brightly while standing on the battlefield encircled by His army and friends, like Lord Indra surrounded by the demigods." (Valmiki Ramayana, Yuddha Kand, 108.34)

Goswami Tulsidas knows it. Shri Hanuman is firmly aware of it as well, as he remains alive in the manifested realm just so that he can regularly remember it, finding the most wonderful pleasure simply by bringing it to the forefront of his consciousness. Agastya Rishi, the jar-born Vedic seer, whose piety is so strong that the vilest rogues and thieves cannot even approach his hermitage, knows it as well. Sita Devi, the daughter of King Janaka, is the most intimately familiar with it, and the three youngest sons of King Dasharatha of Ayodhya are so in knowledge of it that their very lives revolve around it. Shrila Narada Muni sings about it wherever He goes, and the Vedas have celebrated it in their countless hymns and prayers since time immemorial. On the day that gave Dussehra its real meaning, close friends, allies, and even direct enemies got to witness it personally. As He did that day, the lord of creatures, the Supreme Personality of Godhead, protects His devotees, no matter what size or shape they come in and no matter what their plight may be. Whoever should be harassing them and whatever condition the Lord personally finds Himself in, His promise to protect the saints from danger, to deliver them from the calamities caused by the influence of miscreant characters like Ravana, never breaks. On Dussehra, we remember the time when Lord Rama, the Supreme Lord in His form as a warrior prince, was honored and worshiped for His dedication, when His friends rejoiced in His victory, the one that didn't seem possible.

Was the victorious outcome ever in jeopardy? Shouldn't God be capable of handling any situation? How can God's strengths ever be doubted? Does not the sun rise and set every day? Is not the earth humbled by earthquakes, the moon by eclipses, and the living entities by the threefold miseries of life? Knowing that these occurrences are regular, how can anyone think that another person could be inferior or supremely feared? Forgetfulness is one of the defects borne of the propensity to commit mistakes that is found within every human being. Couple this tendency with the influence of time, material nature's most powerful agent for change, and it's not surprising that man would forget about his own fallibility. Moreover, man even forgets that the defects and pains he encounters in his own life apply to everyone else as well. For these reasons, a powerful Rakshasa during the Treta Yuga was feared to be the most powerful ruler in the world, someone who could never be stopped.

Lost in the immediate aftermath of this fiend's reign of terror was the fact that none of his abilities were acquired through his own effort. Ravana was the product of the union between a Rakshasa mother and a brahmana father. A brahmana by quality and work is a person with saintly qualities, someone who is nonviolent, cool-headed, kind and extremely knowledgeable. The brahmana is considered intelligent because he uses whatever information is fed into the computer that is the mind to further the highest aim of life, that of becoming God conscious. A smart person isn't necessarily someone with a high IQ or someone who knows a lot of facts. True intelligence is marked by the ability to utilize whatever information is gathered to further a specific desire. As everyone is born ignorant, all knowledge comes through acquisition. In this sense it's difficult to make comparative assessments of knowledge gathering abilities, for we don't say that one person is better at eating than another person. Whether it takes us a long time to acquire information or a short time, the fact that we have to accept information from external sources shows that every one of us is flawed.

Intelligence is determined by how the information absorbed is used. Brahmanas possess the most valuable knowledge, because they know that the living beings are Brahman, or pure spirit.

Therefore not only is every human being equal in their constitution, but so is every living entity, from the tiny ant all the way up to the denizens of heaven, the celestial figures that are in charge of the various departments of the material creation. The correct Sanskrit term is dehinam, or embodied, to describe the condition of the sparks of Brahman that roam the material land in different body types.

A brahmana surveys everything with an equal vision acquired through austerity, penance and sacrifice. These activities are taken up with a purpose; to remain tied to the Supreme Lord, the origin of Brahman. A Rakshasa, on the other hand, is not very intelligent. They delight in eating animal flesh, including human carcasses, and drinking wine incessantly. Both the spiritualist and the drug addict are looking to escape the influence of the senses that is concomitant with an embodied existence, but the addict finds an illusory escape, one which only sharpens the fangs of the dangerous material senses. The spiritualist, on the other hand, follows authorized methods passed down in the Vedas, the ancient scriptures of India, to remove the teeth from the serpent-like senses. Thus both persons can appear to be exactly the same on the outside, with one feeling perpetual misery from being constantly bitten, while the other lives peacefully in full knowledge of their constitutional position and the spirit soul's superiority over the material energy.

How did a Rakshasa and a brahmana produce a son then? The sage Vishrava was engaged in meditation when he was interrupted by a Rakshasa woman who wanted to bear a child with him. She was sent to Vishrava by her father for this very purpose, as the Rakshasa clan had just been routed out of the beautiful island of Lanka. Vishrava was angered over having his meditation broken, so he cursed the woman to get her wish. She would get a son through him, but that child would be the vilest creature around. When the time of birth came, this son emerged with a ghastly visage having ten heads. He was thus known by names such as Dashanana and Dashagriva.

His influential powers came later on when he propitiated the first created living entity, Lord Brahma. Dashagriva's mother saw that Kuvera, her husband's son begotten through a different woman, was living very opulently due to benedictions he received from the demigods. Therefore she wanted her sons to have the same abilities. She instructed her sons Dashanana, Kumbhakarna and Vibhishana to perform austerities to please Lord Brahma. Kumbhakarna had a slip of the tongue and mistakenly asked for the benediction to be able to sleep for months at a time, while Vibhishana asked to be devoted to piety. Dashanana received amazing strength, invincibility in battle against seemingly every type of creature. He made the mistake of not asking for immunity from human beings. This would cost him later on.

Using his powers for evil, Dashanana went on a reign of terror. After pleasing Lord Shiva, the Rakshasa received the name Ravana, which means one who has a terrorizing roar. Things got so bad because of Ravana's work that the saintly class started worrying that maybe the world had been turned over to evil for good. The rishis residing in the forests not bothering anyone would have their sacrifices interrupted by Ravana and his Rakshasas congregated in Lanka. They would do more than just disrupt the religious practices of the saints. They would kill the saints and then eat their flesh. In this way Ravana proved to be the vilest of creatures, the worst of the worst. The demigods finally petitioned Lord Vishnu, the Supreme Lord in His personal form, to come to earth and deal with the situation. He would descend as a human being so that Ravana would be killed while the boons granted to him by Brahma would stay protected.

God would appear on earth as Lord Rama, the noble, handsome, pious, kind, and dedicated eldest son of the King of Ayodhya, Maharaja Dasharatha. True to his nature, Ravana would find a way to bother even Rama, though the Lord never bothered anyone. Lakshmana, Rama's younger brother, once remarked that even the people punished by Rama could not find fault in Him. This was because they knew that Rama did not play favorites when administering justice, that He never unjustly punished any person. This fact made Ravana's act of taking away Rama's wife Sita all the more vile.

Rama couldn't be defeated by Ravana's 14,000 attacking Rakshasa warriors sent to the forest of Dandaka, and neither would the Lord remain on the sidelines when His wife went missing. Ravana took Sita away through a backhanded plot, which ironically sealed his doom at the same time. Sita's kidnap gave Rama the excuse needed to take on Ravana and thus satisfy the desire of the saintly class. Even with Rama's amazing mastery of archery, His ability to shoot arrows that were like nuclear weapons in strength, there was still some doubt as to the final outcome; such is the nature of embodied living. We know that life will go on after a particular sporting event takes place, but we still get nervous during the critical moments when watching. The air of uncertainty is always there in a land where birth and death take place in repeating cycles.

The uncertainty in the minds of the nervous onlookers was strengthened by the fact that during the final battle between Rama and Ravana, the demon king seemed to be unbeatable. Rama kept lopping off his many arms and heads, and yet Ravana just kept growing new ones. Such amazing creatures aren't seen today, so the historical accounts found in the Ramayana may seem like mythology, but as the saints so nicely point out, the wonderful displays of strength and ability from beings in this world are nothing compared to what God can do. Even the Supreme Lord's personal exhibition of strength represents but a tiny fragment of what He is truly capable of. Therefore it was not that surprising to see Ravana continually regenerate new heads and arms.

Rama's army consisted of monkeys fighting with rocks and uprooted trees, while Ravana's army was full of Rakshasas expert in black magic. It didn't seem like a fair fight, but Rama's side was winning nonetheless. In the final battle, when it seemed like there was no way that Ravana would be killed, that even Rama couldn't defeat him, the Lord took out His most powerful arrow, one passed down from Lord Brahma, a weapon that previously belonged to Agastya Rishi. Chanting the proper mantras as He drew the arrow to His bow, Rama released the powerful weapon, which marked the culmination of the intense struggle with Ravana, an arrow that allayed the fears of the fighting monkeys, the saintly class of men and the celestials watching from above. Penetrating Ravana's body, that arrow ended the demon's life and any chances the Rakshasas had of victory.

After Ravana was slain, Rama's friends and well-wishers fighting for His side congregated around Him and praised His achievement. The scene was reminiscent of Lord Indra, the king of heaven, being surrounded by the celestial fighters after a victory over the asuras, or demons. Up until this point in time Rama had endured so much for others. He went to the forest for fourteen years to maintain the good name of His father, who had promised two boons to his youngest wife Kaikeyi. Rama took Sita and Lakshmana with Him because they insisted on coming along. The Lord fought 14,000 Rakshasas all by Himself to protect the saints in the forests. The Lord killed the monkey-king Vali so that His friend Sugriva would no longer live in fear. He accepted an estranged Vibhishana into His camp and installed him on the throne of Lanka even before Ravana's death. He worshiped the sun-god at the behest of Agastya just prior to the final battle with Ravana, and He even took out His most potent arrow only after His charioteer suggested it.

Dussehra is Rama's day. On that battlefield many thousands of years ago the Lord did away with the most nefarious creature ever to have roamed the sacred earth, and He proved once again that the songs of the Vedas and the words of the saints are not empty, that God does protect those who surrender unto Him in earnest. On Dussehra we remember, honor and cherish Shri Rama in His beautiful form, smiling and holding His bow and arrow. Rama never asks anything from anyone, but if someone is devoted to Him, He promises to stand by them. Because He removes the fears of the devotees, He is known as Hari. Because His name is as powerful as the arrows that fly from His bow, the devotees craving His association regularly chant the holy names, "Hare Krishna Hare Krishna, Krishna Krishna, Hare Hare, Hare Rama Hare Rama, Rama Rama, Hare Hare".

In Closing:

See Rama's face that is always smiling,
In His hands bow and arrow He is holding.

The saints and the innocent He is protecting,
Their honor and fame always worth defending.

Ravana, he of scream that is terrorizing,
Sacrifices of saints he given to destroying.

Received boons from Brahma, lord of creating,
So that none in battle him would be defeating.

Immunity from all creatures he got from asking,
Would pay the price for human beings forgetting.

In the form of Shri Rama, of beauty logic defying,
Would come Ravana's doom, end of life approaching.

Through a fierce fight, after many arrows went flying,
Rama released Brahma's weapon, Ravana's chest penetrating.

Dussehra is day for Rama's glories to be celebrating,
Remember the Lord and His entourage through His names chanting.

DUSSEHRA III

sarvataścābhipetustān vānarā drumayodhinaḥ |
daśagrīvavadhaṃ dṛṣṭvā vānarā jitakāśinaḥ ||

"The Vanaras, who fought using trees, attacked the demons from all sides. Seeing the ten-necked leader killed, the Vanaras assumed a triumphant attitude." (Valmiki Ramayana, Yuddha Kand, 108.24)

If your enemy fights with state of the art weaponry that they are skilled in maneuvering, and you are using basic objects found in nature like trees and rocks, how on earth will you win? You're basically kidding yourself, as you may fight the gallant fight for a while, but eventually the sheer force of the opposition's weaponry will defeat you. Ah, but when you have the Supreme Lord as your leader, you don't need any outside help. You don't even have to be very strong or capable. Just the desire to serve Him is enough, and on the occasion of Dussehra we remember the service of some of the most valiant warriors in history.

Lord Ramachandra is the Supreme Personality of Godhead in His incarnation as a warrior prince. There have been many famous princes in history, but none has been more talked about and celebrated than the eldest son of King Dasharatha of the Ikshvaku dynasty. His glories are sung in the Vedas, which are the oldest scriptures in existence. The ancient Vedic texts like the Ramayana and Shrimad Bhagavatam describe God's qualities in both His incarnations such as Rama and His personal form, and to this day the glorification continues through the saints who have inherited the spiritual tradition of bhakti-yoga from their spiritual masters, who belong to an instructional lineage that originates with the Supreme Lord Himself.

From Shri Rama's life so many lessons can be taken away, including on topics such as administration, defense, pious principles, deference to one's preceptors and parents, and brotherly love. But a higher purpose for coming to earth and gracing the population with His vision is to give the saints something to talk about, something to relish. The mind works all the time, even while we are asleep. Think about that for a second. From the time of your birth up until this very moment your mind has never stopped. It will keep going in the future as well, which means that you'll always have to think about something. It stands to reason then that if the quality of the subject matter of that thought increases, the pleasure from the thinking will increase as well.

God's qualities are inconceivably wonderful, so He is described as nirguna, or without qualities. The nirguna tag is also sometimes used to describe the Lord's unmanifest feature, His presence which is not perceptible to the eye. Conversely, the saguna form is the personal incarnation, but nirguna in a different context means that the gunas, or qualities, belonging to the Lord are all spiritual. They are not binding to the cycle of birth and death as they are with ordinary living entities.

A major act of the real-life play directed by Lord Rama took place in Lanka, an island ruled over by a wicked king named Ravana at the time. Rama didn't just come to earth to go on a killing spree. In fact, His demeanor was the opposite of aggressive. He was very kind and polite and didn't speak much. He followed the direction of His parents and His spiritual guides, which is humorous in a sense, as God doesn't need instruction from anyone. Yet just to set a good example He followed the wishes of the father Dasharatha and the gurus Vishvamitra and Vashishtha. Rama also couldn't help but listen to His wife Sita and His younger brother Lakshmana, who insisted on accompanying Him wherever He went.

When Rama had to live in the forest for fourteen years, they both came along as well, and later on Sita was taken away to Lanka behind Rama's back. Ravana perpetrated this deed, and for this he was worthy of punishment. A mentality opposite of that of Sita and Lakshmana, Ravana had no desire to serve God or even acknowledge His supremacy. Rather, Ravana would amass wealth using his strength and then enjoy his lofty position. But all his hard-earned gains would come crashing down as soon as he decided to try to enjoy the person who is always off-limits. Sita is Lakshmi

Devi, the goddess of fortune, and she serves her husband, Narayana, all the time. Narayana is another name for God, and Rama is the same Narayana.

Ravana wasn't alone in Lanka. He had fellow ogres there with him. They were expert in black magic, similar to witches. They looked ghoulish, and they fought dirty. Previous to Sita's abduction, Ravana's friends had harassed many a sage in the forest. They would attack at night when it was difficult to see, and they would first assume an innocent guise. Just when they got close, they would reveal their true forms and then kill the sages and eat their flesh. These vile creatures were man-eaters who preyed on the most innocent members of society.

Rama one time singlehandedly defeated 14,000 of Ravana's cohorts that were sent towards Him. When the time came for Sita's rescue, Rama teamed up with Vanaras, who are like an advanced race of monkeys. Rama had a more conventional army back home, but due to the stipulations of the exile set by His father's youngest wife Kaikeyi, Rama wouldn't return to Ayodhya for help. No matter, as the Vanaras were sufficiently capable for the job; they possessed the one attribute necessary for victory: devotion.

In the final battle, the Rakshasas used every trick they had, but the monkeys, who were led by Hanuman, held their own. Finally, there was the battle between Rama and Ravana, and when the Lord released the arrow bestowed by Lord Brahma, Ravana was killed. Seeing this, the Vanaras, who were fighting with trees, swarmed the enemy Rakshasas. Rama's army assumed the triumphant attitude because their spirits were uplifted by the Lord's victory. With such high spirits there was nothing the Rakshasas could do.

When you know you are on the side of good and you have the leader of that goodness there to support you, there is no chance of defeat, no matter what the external conditions portend. In the present day and age the enemies live both within and without. Lust, anger and greed attack us on the inside, and the forces intent on denying God's existence ruin society on the outside. Yet weapons of the same potency as the arrows shot by Rama are available to us in the holy names, "Hare Krishna Hare Krishna, Krishna Krishna, Hare Hare, Hare Rama Hare Rama, Rama Rama, Hare Hare". This mantra is the battle hymn of the bhakti army, and chanting it regularly gives the troops the same confidence that the Vanaras had back on that first Dussehra.

In Closing:

Shri Rama, Supreme Lord, has won,
Ravana's reign of terror now done.

Vanaras in victory shout,
Enemy forces they begin to route.

Relying on black magic the demons fought,
Mind-bending illusions to battle they brought.

Rama's army used only rocks and trees,
But on opportunity for service they seized.

From devotion to Rama assured was their victory,
On Dussehra day with smiles we remember their story.

DIWALI I

"Seeing the city of Kishkindha, which was formerly protected by Vali, Sita, who was feeling shy out of love, then spoke the following humble words to Rama: 'O King, I wish to enter Your capital city of Ayodhya with You, accompanied by the beloved wives of Sugriva, headed by Tara, as well as the wives of the other Vanara leaders.'" (Valmiki Ramayana, Yuddha Kand, 123.23-25)

Diwali is the homecoming of homecomings, one of the greatest celebrations ever seen on this earth. We read of festive occasions of the past, wherein excitement and joy were experienced on the grandest scale. Usually these celebrations relate to the victory of a certain king, ruler, or oppressed group of citizens. In the case of Diwali, the celebration deals with the triumphant return of a group of noble characters who were put through the toughest trials and tribulations, experiences that would make even the strongest person buckle. To honor and celebrate their joyous victory and successful return home, the residents of the town of Ayodhya lit many wonderful lamps and placed them around the city. This splendorous scene was so memorable that it spawned an annual celebration known as Diwali, or the festival of lights.

Christmas is celebrated with wonderful decorations and elaborate lighting. Other holidays and festive occasions are celebrated in a similar manner. If we want to be put into a joyous mood, visually appealing surroundings are helpful. Just as putting on a nice set of clothes enhances the presence we convey to others, putting up nice decorations around the house serves as a way to lighten the mood and make visitors feel welcome and happy. Many thousands of years ago, the visitors were actually former residents, members of the royal order. They had been banished from the kingdom for fourteen years prior due to ill fortune and family infighting. Victory never comes easily, especially when life and death are at stake and fighting with demons and the kidnap of a beautiful princess are thrown into the equation. Once exiled, the return of this group was never guaranteed, so the citizens prayed every day and never diverted their thoughts from the lotus feet of their abandoned one, their beloved prince whose birthright was the kingdom. Hearing that He was arriving, the citizens made sure to go all out to welcome Him. Aside from playing nice music and decorating the streets and buildings, the citizens lit lamps, or dipas, as a way to worship their divine leader and His entourage upon their return.

Why were the citizens so attached to this group? Many thousands of years ago, during the Treta Yuga, the world was ruled by a pious king named Dasharatha. He belonged to a famous family of rulers known as the Ikshvakus. Maharaja Ikshvaku himself was one of the first kings on earth, so his descendants all followed his wonderful example of chivalry and dedication to dharma, or righteousness. Yet Dasharatha was saddened because he had no heir to pass the kingdom down to. The Vedas inform us that a man assumes three debts at the time of birth, with one of them being to the forefathers. If it weren't for the great efforts of our parents and grandparents, we could never take birth under the circumstances that we do. Therefore it is incumbent upon men, especially those of the royal order, to repay the favor to their ancestors by begetting sons. This also ensures that the family name continues. If a specific section of society is ruled by a good government, there will generally be peace and tranquility. Dasharatha was fit in every way to be king, but since he had no heir, there was some apprehension about the future.

Through good fortune and the performance of a sacrifice, Dasharatha was blessed with four sons, all of whom were incarnations of the Supreme Personality of Godhead, Lord Vishnu. The eldest son Rama was a direct expansion of Vishnu, so He was fully and completely non-different from God. Rama came to earth for a specific purpose, that of defeating a particularly strong demon named Ravana. Dasharatha was naturally attached to Rama from the time of His birth, but due to divine will, he was forced to part with Rama before he wanted to. Fate is a product of time, which is nature's agent of change. Nature is controlled by the demigods, or the divine figures residing in the heavenly realm. These celestials needed Rama to have an excuse to kill Ravana, so they had to set the wheels in motion for the Lord's exile from Ayodhya. They got what they wanted when Dasharatha's youngest wife, Kaikeyi, suddenly demanded that her son, the younger brother of Rama, Bharata, succeed the king on the throne instead of Rama. In addition, she asked that Rama be sent to live in the forest for fourteen years.

Dasharatha could not prevent these two desires from being fulfilled. He had previously agreed to give Kaikeyi any two wishes of her choosing. Though Dasharatha never could actually give the orders to Rama, the Lord took it upon Himself to execute the will of the queen. As descendants of Ikshvaku, members of the family had a duty to abide by their word. Rama would not allow His father to be made out to be a liar. In addition, Dasharatha had been cursed previously to die as a result of separation from his beloved son. This indeed would occur as the king would give up his life shortly after Rama's departure for the forest.

The Lord took with Him His beautiful wife Sita Devi and His younger brother Lakshmana. Rama was simply required to roam the forests in the garb of an ascetic, but of course His time in the woods would be eventful. Ravana's imminent demise was secured when he hatched a scheme to take Sita away while she was not with Rama and Lakshmana. Seeing that His wife was taken away, Rama travelled the forests and eventually formed an alliance with a monkey king named Sugriva. The Vanaras, monkey-like humans, had taken refuge in the forest of Kishkindha, where Sugriva and his massive army, which included Shri Hanuman, lived. Rama and Lakshmana, forging an alliance with Sugriva, eventually made their way to Ravana's kingdom of Lanka to take on the demon in battle. After fierce fighting and tremendous bravery shown by the monkeys, Rama was able to successfully defeat and kill Ravana. Upon rescuing Sita, the Lord and His closest associates ascended the celestial car, which originally belonged to the demigod Kuvera, and embarked on their journey back to Ayodhya.

At the time, Rama had been separated from Sita for almost a year. Therefore as they were travelling back home on this celestial airplane, the Lord pointed out all the various points of interests relating to His journey. He showed Sita all the places she had not seen due to her kidnap. At one point, Rama showed Sita the forest of Kishkindha, where He forged the alliance with Sugriva and Hanuman. Sita, who is the kindest and sweetest person to have ever graced this earth, in a very shy manner, politely asked Rama if the airplane could stop in Kishkindha to pick up the wives of the monkeys, including Tara, who was Sugriva's wife.

Sita and Rama, being the divine couple and the mother and father of the universe, are always on the same page. Their natures match up perfectly, and this incident is another reminder of that fact. Lord Rama refused to return home to Ayodhya alone. He loved the Vanaras so much because of the selfless devotion they showed to Him. The Supreme Lord is all-powerful, so He doesn't need anyone's help in any endeavor. But since it is the nature of the individual soul to act in God's service, the Lord kindly accepts whatever devotion one shows to Him. The monkeys asked nothing of Rama; they simply served Him due to their pious nature. They had no enmity with Ravana; neither had they even met Sita. But they knew who Rama was, and since He was in trouble, they took His pain to be theirs. These are the workings of love. True love means wanting more for the object of your affection than you want for yourself. The Vanaras met this requirement completely, and their love did not go unnoticed. Rama made sure to fit as many of them as he could onto the celestial car returning to Ayodhya.

Sita Devi, for her part, only really knew Shri Hanuman, Sugriva's faithful minister who had bravely fought off all of Ravana's evil elements and made his way to see Sita prior to the final battle. Sita is forever Hanuman's well-wisher, and since the other monkeys also helped her husband, she had a deep love and respect for them as well. On this return trip home, Sita empathized with the plight of the wives of the monkeys. They had to remain at home while their heroic husbands went to battle one of the greatest demonic forces the world had ever seen. Surely they were deserving of praise and adulation as well. Sita wanted all the wives to come and join in the festivities in Ayodhya. Sita didn't want to celebrate alone. She wanted every person who played even the tiniest of roles in her rescue and her husband's triumph to bask in the glory of victory. Lest there be any doubt on the matter, this incident proves that the

Lord and His consorts never forget even the slightest service that is offered to them with love and devotion.

The Supreme Lord is never alone. When we speak of Rama, Vishnu, and Krishna, their closest associates and family members are included. The Lord is never worshiped alone; His pleasure potency expansions such as Sita, Radha, and Lakshmi are always with Him. In the case of Lord Rama, Lakshmana and Hanuman are also always with the Lord. Just as Rama is worshipable, so is His land of Ayodhya. Just as the land of Ayodhya is worshipable, so are the divine residents who stood vigil for the fourteen years of Rama's exile. Just as the residents of Ayodhya are worthy of praise and respect, so are the selfless Vanaras for their heroic efforts in service of Sita, Rama, and Lakshmana.

On Diwali Day, we remember the Lord and His family. We remember the great homecoming they received and the wonderful services offered to them by their pure devotees. Even if one is unable to understand the divine nature of Sita and Rama, they will still be benefitted by the couple's association. Sita and Rama's characters and behavior resulting from their nature have never been seen since on this earth. Simply hearing of their extraordinary kindness, benevolence, chivalry, bravery, and loving feelings towards all of humanity is enough to purify the heart. If one simply remembers this great scene of the triumphant return of Rama, Lakshmana, and Sita, along with the Vanaras and their family members, they will never fall out of grace with the Supreme Lord and His family. Keeping this divine vision in the mind up until the time of death, the soul will become liberated and return to the transcendental sky, where every day is a festival of lights and every minute brings the divine vision of Sita and Rama.

DIWALI II

hiraṇyanābhan śailendran kāñcanaṃ paśya maithili | |
viśramārthan hanumato bhittvā sāgaramutthitam |

"O Sita, see the golden lord of mountains [Mainaka], which is golden-peaked and which rose up, piercing the ocean, to provide rest to Hanuman." (Lord Rama speaking to Sita Devi, Valmiki Ramayana, Yuddha Kand, 123.18)

Lord Rama, the victorious son of King Dasharatha, having just slain His enemy who had unrightfully taken His religiously wedded wife away from Him, was riding home in the aerial car known as the Pushpaka. An arduous many months had just culminated with the rescue of His wife Sita Devi, and now came the time to go back home, to return to His land where He had not been for fourteen years. The last memories Rama had of that place were from the day He was almost crowned as the new king, with His father King Dasharatha ready to hand the throne over to Him, as He was the eldest son. Fourteen years having passed and Dasharatha having quit His body, Rama would return home nonetheless. He would be received with a tremendous welcome consisting of so many lights that the occasion became celebrated thereafter as Diwali or Deepavali, which means a row of lamps. On the way home, Shri Rama, happy to be reunited with His wife, pointed out to her a collection of important places which were soon to become sacred pilgrimage sites. Always mindful of the services offered to Him, Rama even noted the important areas relating to His dearmost servants, which included the best of them all, Shri Hanuman.

If you haven't seen one of your closest friends for a while, when you do actually meet up with them, you'll want to know what they have been up to. "What have you been doing? What did you do for such and such occasion? How are your friends and family doing?" With Sita, her meeting with Rama piqued an even stronger interest, for she had been held captive in a tucked away grove of Ashoka trees for many months. The wicked ruler of the island kingdom of Lanka had taken her away from the side of her husband and then threatened to kill her if she didn't give in to becoming his wife. Lord Rama is the Supreme Personality of Godhead in the guise of a human being, someone who is spiritual in every way. The fact that Rama is still celebrated to this day and His glorious qualities and activities still studied and taken delight from shows that He is no ordinary human being. The shastras already reveal to us Rama's divinity, but as if we needed further convincing, annual occasions like Diwali remind us that Rama is God not only based on His own displays of strength and valor, but also from the merits of His associates, who substantiate the Lord's supreme position with their every act.

Try to imagine the most beautiful woman in the world and you'll get a slight idea of Sita Devi's appearance. One way that the Vedas, the ancient scriptures of India, describe God is to say that He is the source of all energies. He is also the most fortunate living entity; hence He is known as Bhagavan. One of these fortunes involves having the most beautiful consort by your side. It would make sense then that Rama's wife would be lacking nothing in terms of beauty. Since having her company is one of the greatest rewards in life, she is known as the goddess of fortune. Since God is married to the goddess of fortune, He is known by such names as Shripati, Shrinatha, Madhava, Lakshmipati and Sitapati.

Based on the definitions of Rama's names, Sita cannot be with any other man. It is simply not possible. During her marriage ceremony on earth, many kings came to Janakpur to try to raise the bow handed down by Lord Shiva, which would earn them Sita's hand in marriage. Yet only Shri Rama could lift the bow, as He is the only person worthy of being Sita's husband. The external events always seem to be manageable, that if we can just manipulate things a certain way we'll achieve our end. The Lord's constitutional position, however, is absolute. As spirit souls, we too are knowledgeable, blissful and eternal, but our brilliant qualities can be covered up from time to time based on the type of body we assume. Hence we go through temporary ups and downs, gains and losses. With Rama there is never a loss. Even when it seems otherwise, Rama will rise to the challenge and maintain His constitutional position as the supreme enjoyer and husband of the goddess of fortune.

As if having learned nothing from the contest in Janaka's kingdom, Ravana thought he could have Sita even after she was married to Rama. He took her away through a backhanded plot, for he couldn't survive in a fair fight against Rama. Ravana was proud of his strengths achieved through pleasing divine figures, but he liked his opulence and good standing too much to try to jeopardize them by fighting with someone who he was told could defeat him. Thinking that by taking Sita away Rama would then wallow in despair and not continue to fight, Ravana figured he was safe in Lanka.

"Just as a tree starts to blossom during the proper season, so the doer of sinful deeds inevitably reaps the horrible fruit of their actions at the appropriate time." (Lord Rama speaking to Khara, Valmiki Ramayana, Aranya Kand, 29.8)

Little did Ravana know that Rama doesn't work alone. Just as the rewards of karma come to the worker at the right time -similar to how the trees blossom in season - Ravana's punishment and Rama's reunion with Sita were in the works as soon as the beautiful princess was taken away. Though the odds seemed stacked against Rama - as He was roaming the forest with only His younger brother Lakshmana by His side while Ravana had a massive army in Lanka - the Lord is never bereft of accompanying divine associates. He can even take monkeys and turn them into devoted fighters. Ironically enough, that's exactly what He would do.

How did this transformation happen? As a touchstone turns iron into gold, communion with the divine consciousness turns an individual from any species into a surcharged soul capable of carrying out their devotion to the Supreme Lord. The Vanaras in the kingdom of Kishkindha were guaranteed of success in their mission simply based on their desire to serve Rama. The most capable Vanara was Hanuman, and he would play an integral role in Sita's rescue. The first step in Ravana's demise was learning where he was living, which meant finding where Sita was. It wasn't even known for sure if Ravana had taken her or if Sita was still alive. Therefore a search party had to be sent out to scour the earth, to leave no stone unturned.

Sugriva, the leader of the monkeys in Kishkindha, dispatched his massive monkey army to perform this task, while in the back of his mind he knew that only Hanuman would be able to succeed. Sure enough, the burden would fall upon Hanuman to leap to the island of Lanka once it was learned that Sita was there. Not having an aerial car with him, Hanuman's only option was to jump from a mountaintop and fly across the ocean. Since he was carrying out Rama's work, the celestials in the sky and other powerful figures around the scene watched with rapt attention. The ocean personified was one such onlooker, and he wanted to help Hanuman. The ocean had a link to the Ikshvaku dynasty, the family in which Rama appeared. Hanuman was helping Rama, thus the ocean felt that it should help out someone who was doing work on behalf of the Ikshvakus. Whoever would help Hanuman would also play a part in the sacred sequence of events that would be celebrated for millions of years in the future.

The mountain Mainaka acted on behalf of the ocean. He was told to rise out of the ocean and act as a resting place for Hanuman during his journey. When Hanuman approached, Mainaka revealed what he had been told and how he would be supremely honored to offer at least some service to Hanuman, who was carrying out Rama's business. Hanuman did not want any help though, for he was determined to fly ahead. Nevertheless, since he was asked so nicely, he honored Mainaka and the ocean by touching his hand on the top of the mountain and then proceeding on with his journey.

Shri Rama is antaryami, or the supreme witness, which means that He resides within the heart of every living entity. Therefore He knew what Hanuman was up to, but He still took great delight in hearing about his journey later on. On the trip home to Ayodhya, while riding in the aerial car Rama pointed out the mountain Mainaka to Sita and told her that this was where Hanuman was granted rest in his flight to Lanka. During this trip home, Rama had pointed out to Sita various places where Rakshasas had been killed and other things had taken place relating to her rescue. Sita was in captivity while the final battle was going on, so she really had no information of what transpired. Moreover, she had no idea where the notable events took place.

Rama knew that the victory was a team effort, and He was supremely pleased by the faithful dedication shown by the Vanaras, including Hanuman. For these reasons He thought that the specific locations relating to Hanuman were as important as those relating to His own achievements. From her own observations and the descriptions given to her by Rama, Sita could understand what the Vanaras had sacrificed, and how they were forever devoted to both she and her husband. When Rama later pointed out Kishkindha, Sita asked for the car to stop to pick up the wives of the monkeys, for Sita understood what it was like to be waiting somewhere while your husband was off fighting to the death with a powerful enemy. She wanted the chief Vanaras and their wives to accompany them on the journey home, where they would be ceremoniously greeted.

Diwali reminds us of Rama's triumphant return home and the wonderful service that the Vanaras provided. With Rama come Lakshmana and Sita, and also Hanuman and his many monkey friends. With a transcendental family like that, how can anyone who thinks of them ever feel alone? On the day where they lined up a row of welcoming lights, the faithful residents of Ayodhya would get to see their beloved Rama again, and they would get to hear of the events relating to His fourteen year exile and how Sita was eventually rescued. What they didn't know was that their celebration would itself spark an ageless tradition, one that continues to this very day.

From the journey home and the celebration now known as Diwali, we see that any service rendered to Shri Rama or one of His servants never goes in vain. Every kind act is noticed by Rama Himself, and He takes so much delight from them that He shares His sentiments with Sita, taking great pleasure in being so honored. Therefore it was not surprising that the residents of Ayodhya would lay out a massive collection of lamps to welcome back their beloved Rama. That same Supreme Lord can eternally reside within our minds by regularly worshiping Him and His associates and chanting the holy names, "Hare Krishna Hare Krishna, Krishna Krishna, Hare Hare, Hare Rama Hare Rama, Rama Rama, Hare Hare".

In Closing:

Shri Rama shows to Sita the mountain with golden peak,
Which gave rest to Hanuman while Lanka trying to reach.

The couple returning to Ayodhya, on the way home,
Flying in aerial car with closest friends, never alone.

Sita, captive in Lanka for months that were many,
So seeing places related to rescue made her happy.

Shri Rama Vanaras with Hanuman did help,
Their devotion to the Lord Sita could tell.

Therefore she was happy to see places of significance,
Relating to Hanuman, immeasurable in importance.

With the output of devotion Rama does not bother,
Looks for sincerity only, like Him no other.

Residents of Ayodhya had not seen Him for fourteen years,
Aligned rows of lamps when of His arrival they did hear.

Festival so grand that annual tradition it did spark,
To remember Rama's arrival home, to please the heart.

DIWALI III

tvamasmākaṃ caturṇāṃ vaibhrātā sugrīva pañcamaḥ ||
sauhārdājjāyate mitramapakāro'rilakṣaṇam |

"O Sugriva, you are a fifth brother to us four, for a friend is born of affection, while maleficence is the symptom of an enemy." (Bharata, Valmiki Ramayana, Yuddha Kand, 127.45)

Diwali is an ancient Hindu tradition whose origin is in a blessed event from a long time ago. The first Diwali, or festival of lights, marked a triumph of an unlikely group of individuals who were previously cast into strange and unexpected circumstances. The celebration involved both the victorious and those who were joyous of their victory. In honor of their return to their home, an arrival which included many guests never before seen, the residents of the town of Ayodhya lit many lamps, filling the city with welcoming light. The leader of the city for the period preceding the arrival was likely the happiest person there, and his goodwill extended to the friends of the arriving party.

As a quick background, King Dasharatha was the ruler of the kingdom of Ayodhya. His family history dated back to the beginning of the creation, when King Ikshvaku ruled over the same area. Ikshvaku was a king of the utmost character. He did not have any sin in him, and for this he was worthy of the post of ruler of the earth. Several generations down the line Dasharatha took over. He proved his fighting ability on the battlefield, and so under his leadership the citizens felt safe from enemy attack.

In the fourth stage of his life Dasharatha finally had sons, four of them in fact. The eldest Rama was the most beloved of all. He was to succeed the father, but on the day slated for His coronation, events took a dramatic turn in the opposite direction. Due to the influence of the youngest wife Kaikeyi, Dasharatha's commitment to the truth was used against him. He was forced to pass over Rama and give the throne to Kaikeyi's son Bharata. Rama was okay with this, as He held tremendous affection for His three younger brothers. But then Kaikeyi also demanded that Rama be banished from the kingdom for fourteen years. Again, Rama took this in stride, but the rest of the town did not. They were sad to see Him leave, and so through the subsequent fourteen years they waited with great anticipation for His return.

Just imagine living in royal opulence one day and complete squalor the next. And mind you, the squalor is not for just a day or two. It is to last for fourteen years. Rama was accompanied by His beautiful wife Sita in the forest. The younger brother Lakshmana also came. Rama didn't ask them to come along; they insisted. So the forest wasn't so bad for the trio, as they had each other. Sita's company is the most preferable for Rama, and who wouldn't want a powerful and dedicated brother like Lakshmana around?

This stay in the forest was not to be without hiccups, however. Hardship came when Sita was kidnapped by the Rakshasa fiend Ravana, the king of the island of Lanka. Though without His royal army to support Him, Rama still fought ahead to find His missing wife. He aligned with Vanaras in the Kishkindha forest through the help of a minister named Hanuman. Vanaras are similar to monkeys except they have human-like features as well. These events took place in the Treta Yuga, which is the second time period of creation. During that time even the forest dwellers with tails had some semblance of civilized behavior in them.

Hanuman worked for Sugriva, who was the leader of the monkeys stationed on Mount Rishyamukha. Sugriva had his own issues, separated from his family due to a feud with his more powerful brother Vali. Since Sugriva was now a friend, and since Hanuman was trusted as an ally upon initial meeting, Rama agreed to help Sugriva regain his kingdom. Later on Sugriva repaid the favor, first sending Hanuman to look for Sita and then joining the Vanara army in the march to Lanka to rescue her. They would emerge victorious, as the Vanaras had devotion to Rama, which was all that was required. The opponents fought with jaw-dropping illusion and mighty weapons, but with their trees and rocks Sugriva's army countered them. Rama and Lakshmana took care of the rest.

The trio of Rama, Lakshmana and Sita were set to triumphantly return home to Ayodhya, taking an aerial car originally belonging to the treasurer of the demigods, Kuvera. Of course Rama was not going to return home without His friends who had helped Him. Sugriva, Hanuman and the leading Vanaras from the army were invited on to the aerial car to return to Ayodhya. Sita also made sure that the wives of these Vanaras were picked up along the way so that they could enjoy the celebration as well.

Meanwhile, on the other side of things the younger brother Bharata eagerly awaited the return of Rama. He felt terrible for what his mother had done, and so he ruled the kingdom in Rama's absence through a life of asceticism. Rama's sandals were symbolically ruling over the kingdom, and Bharata worshiped those sandals day and night. Before finally arriving home, Hanuman was sent to meet with Bharata, to see what his mindset was. Perhaps he wouldn't want to give the kingdom back to Rama.

Hanuman learned that Bharata had no intention of keeping the kingdom he never wanted. The devoted brother was delighted to see Rama return. He paid his respects to Rama, and then offered respect to Sita and Lakshmana. Bharata then embraced Sugriva and the Vanaras. He kindly told Sugriva that he considered him to be like a fifth brother in their family of four brothers. He said that friends are made through affection and enemies through ill will. Sugriva had affection for Rama, and so he was automatically a friend to Bharata.

This was the same principle adopted by the residents of Ayodhya, as they were thrilled to see Rama's new friends. They loved Rama so much, so they naturally loved anyone who was dear to Him. The Vanaras are forever dear to Rama, who is the Supreme Lord in His incarnation as a warrior prince. It is certainly beneficial to harbor affection for God, but to meet and honor the devotee is considered more beneficial. Through honoring the devotee the Supreme Lord is pleased even more. Bharata didn't require this instruction; he immediately felt affection for Rama's newest devotees, who were headed by Sugriva. Sugriva risked his life and wellbeing for Rama's sake, and his efforts helped the group successfully return to Ayodhya. On Diwali we remember the Supreme Lord and His closest friends and how they joyfully celebrated in the wonderful homecoming.

In Closing:

"We are brothers numbering four,
Shri Rama all of us adore.

You, Sugriva, hold the same affection too,
Thus as a fifth brother we consider you.

Through affection a friend is born,
And enemies through ill will and scorn."

When the triumphant to Ayodhya returned,
Sight of Rama's new friends residents earned.

Diwali celebration our spirits to uplift,
Meeting with devotee most precious gift.

GOVARDHANA PUJA I

According to the Vedic seers, those who spent much time in samadhi [divine trance], this material world can trace its origin to the desire of the individual souls to imitate their Supreme Master. Similar to how a child desires to imitate the adult activities of its parents, the autonomous spirit souls, who are full of free will and independence, choose to challenge the Supreme Lord in the areas of creation, maintenance, and destruction. To facilitate this desire, God, the original Divine Being, creates a temporary and perishable world wherein the imitators are allowed to roam free. Gaining release from this flawed mindset is quite difficult, so it takes many lives on earth to achieve perfection in a spiritual sense. There are different gradations of transcendentalists, some of whom are further along in the purification process than others. Yet even for those who are on a higher level, the personal assistants of God, breaking free of the challenging spirit is not easy. These elevated personalities often fall victim to their puffed up ego borne of unlimited passions and perceived abilities. To grant His mercy to His closest associates, and also those who depend on the Lord for everything, Shri Krishna, the Supreme Personality of Godhead, enacts wonderful pastimes on this earth, one of which involves the lifting of a giant hill. This pastime and its associated religious rituals are so famous that they are honored every year on the occasion of Govardhana Puja.

God can most certainly come to earth. As the origin of life, He is free to act as He wishes. The CEO is the boss of the company; no one can tell them what to do. Since God is the original boss, no one can force Him to live by any rules that are created for others. For instance, a human being requires a womb and a mother to take birth. Similarly, death is also a requirement for life. For the definition of a life to be valid, there must be both birth and death. For the Supreme Lord, such restrictions are not applicable. He can appear out of any object or person, and He can remain forever in a particular body if He chooses. In His original form, the Lord possesses a transcendental body, something not conceivable to the human brain. When we think of a body, we conjure up a form which is created, remains for some time, and then ultimately decays. Moreover, the functions of this body are limited. Hands can only do certain things; legs can only help one walk and run, the brain can only think, etc. With the Supreme Lord, such body parts are transcendental and thus capable of performing any function. The Supreme Lord, in the body of a young child, can lift an enormous mountain and hold it up without any effort for seven consecutive days. This is precisely what He did during one famous incident; a pastime which reminded everyone, including the demigods in the spiritual sky, of the Lord's supreme power and benevolent nature.

Around five thousand years ago, Krishna descended to earth in His original, transcendental form. Usually when God comes to earth, He does so as an avatara. An avatara means one who descends; hence it refers to the Supreme Lord and His innumerable appearances on earth. Though Krishna is often listed as an avatara of Lord Vishnu, the Supreme Godhead possessing four hands and an opulent appearance, the Lord actually exists eternally on the spiritual planet of Krishnaloka. When Krishna came to earth, He spent His childhood years in the farm community of Vrindavana. Since the time period was so long ago, it shouldn't surprise us that agriculture was a mainstay of society. Even as recently as one hundred years ago, almost forty percent of the workforce in America was involved in agriculture.

In the Vedic tradition, the farmers are part of the division of society known as the vaishyas. Not to be confused with a simple caste based off birthright, vaishyas have specific duties entrusted to them, one of which is cow protection. The cow represents the best kept secret of the economics field. By simply owning and properly taking care of a cow, one can take great strides towards eliminating poverty. The protected animals belonging to the farming community in ancient times proved to be the original "cash cows", with one's wealth even being determined by how many cows they owned. This may seem silly, as a cow is simply an animal, but if one owned a small plot of land with a few cows, there would be no chance of famine or poverty. The greatest fear for any family is to lose their source of income and thus have no way to put food on the table. The cow solves this problem by freely supplying milk, which can then be transformed into varieties of dishes.

Lord Krishna, growing up under the care of His foster parents Nanda Maharaja and Mother Yashoda, would regularly go out to the pasturing grounds and tend to the cows. In India, the rainy season is especially important, as all the nutrition needed for the grains, the source of life, is provided during a few months of the year. One time after the rainy season, Krishna noticed His father preparing for a grand sacrifice, or religious ritual. Inquiring into the matter, Krishna was informed by Nanda Maharaja as to the purpose of the sacrifice. "Lord Indra, the king of heaven, supplies us all of our necessities in the form of rain, which comes from the cloud. Were it not for Indra's mercy, we would not be able to sustain our livelihoods. Therefore we are preparing to worship Indra through a grand sacrifice".

Hearing these words from His father, Krishna decided there was an opportunity to play with Indra's pride. As mentioned before, this pride, which is known as false ego, is the single root cause behind the existence of the material world. The demigods, or celestials, can be thought of as saints or angels. They have bodies which possess extraordinary powers, but since they too must suffer through birth and death, they are deemed conditioned. A liberated soul is one who remains in a spiritual body at all times in the company of the Supreme Lord. In order to come to the material world, a pure soul must become conditioned by the modes of nature. The demigods, though living mostly in goodness, can still fall victim to false ego from time to time. Lord Krishna wanted to play a little trick on His dear friend Indra, while at the same time purifying him of his false ego.

In response to Nanda's words, Krishna said that the hills and mountains were the real sources of sustenance. As agriculturists, the residents of Vrindavana were supported by the cows more than anything else. The cows would graze on the nearby mountains, so if anyone was deserving of worship, it was the neighboring hills, Govardhana Hill in particular. Delighted by the cogent words of his beautiful son, Nanda Maharaja did not raise any opposition. He instructed all the residents to instead direct their preparations and offerings to Govardhana Hill. A wonderful ceremony was performed, with charity and food given to the brahmanas, the priestly class of men. At the end of the ceremony, Shri Krishna, assuming the person of Govardhana Hill, kindly spoke to the residents and informed them of His satisfaction. Lord Krishna, in His original childhood form, at this time also offered obeisances to Himself in the form of Govardhana Hill.

Lord Indra, watching the festivities from his perch in heaven, was not happy at all at this turn of events. Seeing that his sacrifice was neglected, he decided to exact revenge on the residents. He called for his trusted aide, a personified cloud named Samvartaka, to deluge the town with water. Indra gave his assurance that he would aid in the process by creating a giant storm. Following through on the plans, Indra sent forth a torrential downpour on the residents who had just worshiped Govardhana Hill. The winds were howling, and the water levels started to rise rapidly. The cows were especially affected. Mothers tried to protect their calves to the best of their abilities, but they saw many of their babies floating away in the high waters. Having no other recourse, the cows and residents of the town took complete shelter of Krishna. They prayed to Him to protect them.

It should be noted here that the residents did not pray to Indra to forgive them, nor did they feel remorse over having neglected his worship. They were in the direct presence of the Supreme Personality of Godhead, who was the jewel of Vrindavana, the supreme object of pleasure to all the residents, young and old. Krishna had performed many wonderful feats previously, so the residents knew that only He was capable of saving everyone from this most troubling weather event.

As the deluge was wreaking havoc, Lord Krishna stepped in and picked up the giant Govardhana Hill. Taking it as an umbrella, the Lord placed the hill above His head and held it up with one finger. Krishna informed the residents and cows to come under the shelter of the hill and to not worry about its massive weight. Krishna assured them that the hill would not fall as long He was there.

Following the Lord's directive, the residents were rescued by remaining underneath the giant umbrella-like hill for seven consecutive days. When the rain finally stopped, the residents returned to the town, and Krishna replaced the giant hill where it was before.

Indra, feeling remorse over his actions, kindly appeared before Krishna and offered his obeisances. In his prayers, Indra stated that Krishna had now solidified himself as the protector of the cows. He was completely worthy of the names of Gopala and Govinda, which mean one who gives pleasure and protection to the cows and the senses. Lord Krishna, the most merciful and kind-hearted of souls, was satisfied with Indra's prayers. While it is easy to criticize Indra for his transgression, we should remember the the king of heaven is the dearmost friend of the Lord. Krishna, the ultimate reservoir of pleasure, derives great enjoyment from associating with His friends. Therefore the pastimes of the lifting of Govardhana Hill and the quelling of Indra's pride are both sources of pleasure to Krishna and His devotees.

After pacifying Krishna in this way, Indra asked for one more favor. He informed the Lord that a son of his was roaming the earth at the time. This son was none other than Arjuna, the brave warrior of the Pandava family and cousin to Krishna. Indra asked that Krishna kindly protect Arjuna at all times. Krishna replied that He most certainly knew who Arjuna was and that it was His plan to rid the earth of the burden felt by the sinful elements of society. Krishna gave Indra the benediction that Arjuna would never meet with defeat while the Lord remained on the earth. He promised Indra that Arjuna and his four brothers would emerge victorious from a future war that would see the death of millions. Thus satisfied, Indra returned to heaven, and Krishna continued His wonderful childhood pastimes in Vrindavana.

Govardhana Puja has been celebrated annually ever since the festival was inaugurated by Krishna. Just as Krishna is worshipable, so is His land. The Lord confirmed through His own actions that Govardhana Hill was a direct manifestation of Himself, and since this hill still exists in Vrindavana, devotees view it as the most sacred of pilgrimage sites. Around the world, devotees celebrate the Govardhana Puja each year by erecting mock hills made of halva and other nice food preparations. After the ceremony, the wonderful prasadam represented by pieces of the hill is enjoyed by all. By regularly remembering Krishna, His transcendental form, and His wonderful pastimes aimed at pleasing His devotees, we will be able to shift our disposition from challenger of God, to that of lover of God. If this loving attitude remains with us up until the time of death, our liberation from the cycle of birth and death will be assured.

GOVARDHANA PUJA II

There are vengeful gods. There are heavenly personalities who get angry at those who neglect their worship, especially when the neglecting worshipers think deep down that they are making a mistake. There are divine figures who give rewards to their worshipers but then later punish the same people if they should happen to surpass them in areas of opulence, which include beauty, strength and knowledge. The Lord of Lords, the Supreme Personality, however, is complete in Himself. Therefore when He asks us to surrender unto Him, the recommendation is there to provide pleasure for both sides. The neglect of that worship is itself a punishment, for the worshiper misses out on the association of the most blissful entity. Just to show that no harm can come from fully surrendering to Him, the Supreme Person explicitly protects those who abandon other worshipable figures, the ones that get angry at them for neglecting their worship. The occasion of the first Govardhana Puja very nicely proved this fact.

What would a young boy know about religion? If anything, he will probably look for ways to get out of attending religious functions. "Do I have to go? Why does God make us do these things all the time? Can't you and Dad just do it and I'll go do something else?" Forcing the children to participate in spiritual functions is a good way to get them exposed to the sublime life of connecting with God on a regular basis. There must be coercion with children, for that comes with the territory if you want to be a guardian. If children are forced into studying, eating, and sleeping on time, why then should they not be coaxed into attending religious ceremonies?

The common lack of affinity for religious life within young children makes the request that came from Nanda Maharaja's son seem all the more puzzling. Nanda was the king of a small farm community known as Vrindavana. The residents lived off of the grains produced on the land and the milk products produced by the cows. The cows were equal residents of the community; therefore the land belonged to them as well. From their grazing not only were the calves fed milk, but so were the residents of the community. As the cows were well protected and loved by the children, including Nanda's own son Lord Krishna, they produced heaps of milk products, so much so that there was enough of a surplus to sell in the neighboring town of Mathura.

As a pious soul following the recommendations of the priestly class of men, the brahmanas, Nanda made sure to observe the annual rituals aimed at pleasing the devas, or gods. We can think of a deva to be like a department head in a government administration. Similar to paying the tax collector, giving homage to the devas in charge of the various elements of material nature ensures that there is enough rainfall and that pains in life are limited. In one particular year, Nanda Maharaja was preparing for the annual Indra-yajna, or sacrifice offered to Lord Indra, the king of the heavenly planets. Providing rain is one of Indra's duties, which he does after receiving his share of the sacrifices made in his honor. A yajna is a sort of formal religious ritual where offerings are made in a ceremony that has a fire pit at the center. The remnants of the yajna are known as shishta and are considered free of sin.

Aside from the benefit explicitly tied to the specific yajna performed, there is the gradual shift in consciousness that results in the worshipers. The animal community lives off of the same grains that grow from the rain provided by Indra, yet they do not perform any specific worship. This means that the material nature is ready to supply everyone whatever they want and that the human form of life is meant more for advancing in consciousness. As the second grade classroom is important in molding the thinking abilities of the young student to eventually be able to think rationally as an adult, the many yajnas prescribed for the honor of the devas are meant to keep the human being tied to spiritual life, to help him break free of the possessive mentality inherited at the time of birth. We come into this world with nothing and we leave with nothing, so what do we really own?

As the Indra-yajna seemed rather benign, Nanda was a little surprised that his young son Krishna started asking questions about it. Typically, you'd expect your children to ask about a yajna so that they could find ways to get out of attending it, but with Krishna the interest was a little different. After hearing about why the sacrifice was taking place, Krishna suggested that the same preparations be used to worship the neighboring Govardhana Hill, which was supplying so much to the community with its grass. The cows were pleased with the hill, and once the cows were pleased the rest of the community thrived as a result. Therefore why shouldn't there be a celebration for the hill instead?

Charmed by his son's words, Nanda eventually relented. "Why not please Govardhana Hill? Sounds like a good idea." Nanda then suggested that since the preparations were already made for Indra-yajna, they should do two sacrifices, one for each. Amazingly, Krishna rejected this idea. What could be wrong with offering Indra his share and then worshiping Govardhana Hill? Through His yoga-maya potency, Krishna had hidden His real divinity, His standing as the Supreme Lord. Yajna is actually another word for Vishnu, who is known as the chief deva, or deva vara. Vishnu is the same Krishna, which means that following the Lord's insistence in this case would actually favor Nanda Maharaja and the residents of Vrindavana more so than any other kind of worship.

Though Vishnu is Yajna, if the specific sacrifice isn't directly meant to please Him, the full benefit to the worshiper is not there. What does this mean exactly? Material rewards are as temporary as the body types accepted by the spirit soul. Asking for temporary things like rain and good fortune really have no standing with Vishnu, who is replete with transcendental qualities. The true benefit of worshiping God is gaining His association, being able to bask in His sweet vision. A yajna for a demigod is a sort of indirect worship, where Vishnu is essentially pleased but doesn't reveal His full association to the devotee who is not even asking to receive it.

The decision was made, at the insistence of Krishna, that Govardhana Hill would be worshiped that year instead of Indra. On the one side you had Indra, the king of heaven, and on the other you had a hill, which was a collection of earthly elements. Was not the choosing of the latter a little strange? Govardhana Hill was Krishna's proxy on earth, a way to directly accept the offerings of the devoted residents of Vrindavana. The residents would be worshiping Krishna's hill at the Lord's insistence. After creating a wide variety of sumptuous preparations and offering them to the hill, Krishna Himself assumed the role of the hill and spoke to the residents, telling them that He was pleased with their offering. Worship of Govardhana Hill was thus totally in the mood of bhakti-yoga, or devotional service, which is not tainted with material motives.

As if to give us a further reminder of why the worship of Govardhana Hill was the right move, Lord Indra became outraged that his sacrifice was neglected on this particular year. Lord Vishnu does not succumb to the temptations of jealousy. If He did, He would be perpetually angry, as practically every spirit soul roaming the material universe has chosen a worshipable figure that is not He. The atheists worship material nature and the senses, the monists the impersonal effulgence known as Brahman, the yogis the process of meditation and the plenary expansion of the Lord residing within the heart, and the spiritually inclined materialist the many devas, or demigods, capable of offering benedictions. If Vishnu were to give way to jealousy, He would have a lot to be jealous about.

Part of being God means that You don't require anyone's respect. Rather, the master-servant relationship is already part of the constitutions of both parties. This means that serving God is our ideal position, and should we neglect that worship the punishment will automatically come. If we use a fork to try to eat soup, we will have great difficulty. The spoon, not the fork, is made to be used with soup. Similarly, the soul is made to be tied to Krishna in a mood of loving devotion kept alive with constant service. If the soul's eternality, bliss and knowledge are used to further other purposes, the results are not pleasant.

Indra released an onslaught of rain upon the residents as revenge for their transgression. It should be noted that Lord Indra is in great favor with Lord Vishnu, as are all the devas in the heavenly planets. If our children should make a mistake, we don't hold it against them for too long, for our love for them washes away the anger that arises from disappointment. In a similar manner, Krishna's love for

Indra is unbroken, but in this particular incident He decided to teach both Indra and many future generations of listeners a valuable lesson.

That the devas would strike back against people that worshiped them previously was also not out of the ordinary. In his Kavitavali, Goswami Tulsidas remarks that there is no master like Lord Rama, who is the same Vishnu but in a different personal form. Tulsidas notes that other devas grant benedictions for as long as you worship them, but as soon as you rise a little in stature, they get jealous and come after you, trying to take you down from your prestigious position. Shri Rama is not like this, for He appreciates even the most insignificant act of devotion made with sincerity, so much so that he'll often give His devotees a more exalted position.

Indra's jealousy was rooted in the fact that his worship was neglected and that the residents of Vrindavana were following this young boy's advice. The subsequent onslaught of rain instigated by Indra's samvartaka cloud caused an immediate flooding. It would have been understandable for the residents of the town to get angry at Krishna and Nanda Maharaja. "Not only did we neglect to worship Indra, but he is punishing us as a result. This is what we get for listening to Krishna."

But this was not their attitude. Rather, the residents had seen Krishna's ability to save them from danger before. Therefore they instinctively looked to Him to save them again. And rescue them He would. Taking the same Govardhana Hill that was just worshiped, Krishna lifted it up and held it above His head with His tiny finger. Acting as a massive umbrella, the hill provided shelter to the residents, who were thus saved from the massive flooding in Vrindavana. That a young child could lift a massive hill like this and hold it up over His head sounds amazing, but for Krishna it is all part of a day's work. The story of the lifting of Govardhana Hill hints at mythology, but then so do the changing of seasons and the rising and setting of the sun to the young child. If a massive solar body can continually effuse heat and light for billions of years without requiring an external energy source, why should not

Krishna, the creator of the sun, be able to lift up a hill and hold it over His head?

A defeated Indra relented with the rain and then approached Krishna to offer His prayers of contrition. The worship of Govardhana Hill subsequently became an annual tradition, for not only does it please Krishna, it also reminds us of His lifting of the massive hill, which earned Him the name Girivaradhari. There are jealous men and vengeful gods, but Krishna is always in ananda, or bliss. Those who connect with Him by regularly chanting His names, "Hare Krishna Hare Krishna, Krishna Krishna, Hare Hare, Hare Rama Hare Rama, Rama Rama, Hare Hare", and observing His festivals will be granted the same protection that was afforded Nanda and his community.

In Closing:

In Indra-puja, to king of heaven items to offer,
In return rain upon the land does he confer.

Krishna had another idea in mind,
Indra a lesson from episode would find.

The young boy told His father to worship the hill,
The stomachs of the lovely cows with grass did it fill.

Nanda liked the idea but had already prepared,
For Indra-yajna, a most extravagant affair.

Asked Krishna to be able to do both,
Puja for Indra and hill they would hold.

Upon only Govardhana worship did the Lord insist,
Nanda gave in, for on love of son did he subsist.

Though the ceremony was completely religious,
At ignoring his worship did Indra become jealous.

From his anger harboring bad blood,

Vrindavana with rain did he flood.

Fear not for Krishna saved the day by lifting massive hill,
Worshiped as Girivaradhari to this day is He still.

Indra felt sorry for what he did, that he lost his cool,
Forgot Krishna's position, acted like a fool.

Lord was pleased with Indra and his words,
Not angered by the commotion he stirred.

Rely only on Krishna, who accepts loving devotion,
Depend on no other, for He provides all protection.

GOVARDHANA PUJA III

Worship of the Supreme Lord in the mood of bhakti, or divine love, is not like any other kind of interaction. There are benefits for both parties involved, and there is no expectation of reciprocation. The activity falls into a unique category of spirituality, where the temporary conditions fixed in duality are nonexistent. All other varieties of worship can be abandoned in favor of pure, unmotivated and uninterrupted love for God. Aside from the security blanket of unending nectar in the form of the Supreme Lord's association, there is also insulation from the obstruction of outside forces, which include those managed by the higher authorities. Govardhana Puja reminds us of this security, and it also serves to glorify the protector Himself, Shri Krishna.

The miseries of life are threefold. There are those rooted in the body and mind. I know that I shouldn't be sad that my cheating wife has left me, but I can't help it. I can't help but feel inferior, that I'm not good enough. I also know that I shouldn't worry about the outcome to the test I just took, because what can worrying really do? I already took the test, so I either passed or failed. What I think now doesn't matter, yet I can't stop thinking about it. Add diseases to the body and you get the full scope of the miseries the Vedas describe as adhyatmika.

Then there are the adhibautika miseries, those caused by other living entities. Not everyone is nice. Some people are kind and gentle, while others don't mind committing the worst crimes to get what they want. Sometimes they are so mired in a life of ignorance that they don't understand that what they're doing is bad. Such miscreants are a great source of trouble in society.

The adhidaivika miseries are those that we seemingly can't explain. Who causes earthquakes? What about the heat wave that sweeps across the country? And don't forget the torrential downpours which lead to massive flooding. According to the Vedic tradition, the divine figures residing in the heavenly realm are in charge of these forces, and so to keep the resultant miseries at bay one is advised to perform sacrifice. A long time ago, however, the annual sacrifice in honor of the king of heaven, who is in charge of the rain, was skipped. Only for one moment was the sacrifice neglected, and the superior party instantly turned from a friend to an enemy.

Such occurrences are common outside the realm of spirituality as well. We pay homage to the utilities company so that they will provide us electricity. We pay the cable bill so that we'll get the channels we want on our television set. The people we deal with may even be very friendly to us, acting as if our company is enjoyable to them. When we sit down in a restaurant and order food the waiter or waitress may try to act as if we're not there as a customer. The car dealership salesman can also try to act as our friend.

But what if we were to say that we couldn't pay?

"Oh, don't mind me. I'm just sitting here. I'm actually very hungry. Can you bring me some food? I'll have this and that off the menu. And, by the way, I don't have any money with me. I can't afford the prices for these items."

Would the cordial relationship continue? Would not the restaurant owner tell us to leave? Would not the car salesman immediately turn away? In many instances our dealings with divine figures follow the same line, and though we think we are acting in a pious way, we are more or less conducting a business transaction. The desire to earn a profit is there in both parties. The seller wants to make some money on the sale and the buyer doesn't want to spend more than they think the product is worth. The seller a long time back got so angry when a group of innocent people voluntarily decided to take their business elsewhere. They had no need to worry, as their director was the Supreme Lord Himself, the owner of this and every other creation in existence.

In Vrindavana Lord Indra was worshiped annually by the residents. They would gather items for sacrifice and then have a formal worship ceremony, where a priest would consecrate the area and carefully offer each item for Indra's enjoyment. In return Indra would provide the rain necessary to sustain the farm community. One year, Nanda's son decided that the neighboring Govardhana Hill should be worshiped instead of Indra. Nanda was the leader of the community, and his son the jewel of it. Though only a young boy, His attractiveness captivated the hearts and minds of all the residents. Through clever logic and a charming smile, Krishna was able to convince Nanda to shift the preparations towards Govardhana Hill instead.

Spiritual life relates to the spirit soul, which is the essence of identity. This soul is not tied to a material form, nor to any governing commission. In real connection to the Divine, there is no requirement that one follow this behavior or that, or belong to this institution or that. To teach this lesson to Vrindavana's population and to future generations, Krishna purposefully stoked Indra's wrath. The residents didn't have to worship Indra, even if it was standard tradition. Worship of the demigods is a legitimate practice that is mentioned by Krishna Himself in the Bhagavad-gita.

Though a recommended practice for one trying to elevate to a higher consciousness, demigod worship is in essence a business transaction, which means that there is a temporary result, a kind of profit, that comes to both parties. However, the ultimate system of spirituality can never be dependent on a ritual involving personal profit. As soon as the residents changed their mind and worshiped something else, Indra became angry. This means that he wasn't really in it for the benefit of the devotees. He wanted his share, his moment in the spotlight. Once that was gone, envy took over, and instead of leaving the citizens alone, he decided to try to harm them.

Indra instigated a terrible rainstorm upon Vrindavana. Krishna knew that it was Indra's work because the heavy pieces of ice and strong wind were not in season. This was an adhidaivika misery, but since Krishna is the Supreme Lord, it would have no effect on Him or His devotees. The Lord decided to hold up the just worshiped Govardhana Hill using His pinky finger. He held it above His head for seven consecutive days, giving the innocent residents shelter from Indra's wrath.

If the car salesman runs after you with a hammer when you say that you won't buy a car from him, was it worth going to him in the first place? Would you recommend him to others? Worship of Krishna at the highest level is known as bhakti-yoga, or devotional service. It is a voluntary effort, and the only pain that results from neglecting it is the missed opportunity to associate with the reservoir of sweetness, Shri Krishna. The association is the reward in bhakti, and for this reason the truly wise souls abandon all varieties of motivated religious behavior in favor of surrender to God, which they carry out daily by chanting the holy names, "Hare Krishna Hare Krishna, Krishna Krishna, Hare Hare, Hare Rama Hare Rama, Rama Rama, Hare Hare". And as a way to further honor Shri Krishna, the protector of the surrendered souls, they also perform the Govardhana Puja each year on the day after Diwali.

In Closing:

Indra, in a playful pastime involved,
In which Krishna deadly problem solved.

Offerings to king of heaven annually went,
In return vital rain to Vrindavana was sent.

One year the residents worship skipped,
Switch of rage in Indra then flipped.

Devotion to Krishna they all had,
So able to survive Indra's rage mad.

With Govardhana held up in the air,
Krishna removed flooding's scare.

All other varieties of religion forget,
And on loving Krishna keep your heart set.

ABOUT THE AUTHOR

The author, Sonal Pathak, can be contacted through email: **info@krishnasmercy.org**

Other Krishna's Mercy titles from the same author:
Liberty and Dharma
Seeing With Knowledge
God Is Glorious
Praised by Parrots
The Delight of Vrindavana
Free From Karma
Hear to Believe
Devotion Without Obstruction
Devotional Service
Chanting the Holy Names
Hanuman Spotting Sita
To The Worthy Recipient
Worshiping the Deity
Attaining Yoga
Hanuman Enters the Ashoka Grove
Yashoda's Son
Who Else But Hanuman
Hanuman Searches for Sita
Hanuman Entering Lanka
Hanuman Crossing the Ocean
Trusting Hanuman
Welcoming Rama
Lifter of Mountains
Forever Rama's
Devoted to Rama
Lord Rama: The Shelter for the Saints
Meeting Hanuman
Subduer of Enemies
Caught Butter Handed
How We Met: Sita Describing Her Marriage to Rama
Questions About Krishna
The Sharpest Knife: Lakshmana and His Words of Wisdom